Book Promotion for the Shameless

101 Marketing Tips That Really Work

(Revised, 2nd edition)

by Lorna Tedder

With a special bonus section by Internet marketing guru, Jim Daniels

Spilled Candy Books for Writers #2

Spilled Candy Books for Writers, Niceville, Florida

Book Promotion for the Shameless, Copyright 1999, 2001
By Lorna Tedder

Bonus Section copyrighted, Jim Daniels of JDD Publishing

Published by:

Spilled Candy Books for Writers
Spilled Candy Publications
Post Office Box 5202
Niceville, FL 32578-5202
Staff@spilledcandy.com
http://www.spilledcandy.com

Spilled Candy books is committed to its authors and their work. For this reason, we do not permit our covers to be "stripped" for returns, but instead, we require that the whole book be returned in saleable condition, allowing us to resell it. Resaleable is defined as no markings, stamps, scuffs, bent covers, or any condition in which you yourself would not wish to buy the book.

2nd edition, September 2001
Printed in the United States of America
Cover art by Animation Factory.
ISBN:1-892718-01-4 (Disk/Download format)
ISBN:1-892718-38-3 (Paperback)
Library of Congress Catalogue Card Number 99-90258

TABLE OF CONTENTS

Plus 5 FREE articles by Internet marketing guru Jim Daniels to help you start promoting online!

Other Writing and Marketing Guides by Lorna Tedder

Reclaiming the Magic

Book Promotion Savvy

Advanced Book Promotion for the Shameless

Find them all at

http://www.spilledcandy.com

Introduction

Since 1995, the Spilled Candy newsletter has offered terrific tips on book promotion, geared especially to authors who are self-published, small press published, and under-advertised. Over the years, we've have spilled our candy—our wonderful promotion ideas—and other authors have taken those ideas and adapted them to their own books and promotion strategies.

The Spilled Candy newsletter has included both mundane and totally bizarre book promotion ideas that really work. We've seen everything from how to write a press release that really works to how a non-fiction author used his demon possession worker's compensation injury as a publicity hook. Some of the wonderful tips published in the newsletter won't work for you, but most of them can be adapted to whatever type of book you're selling, your personality type, your schedule, and your budget.

So go ahead: enjoy some of the great ideas from our staff and from some of our favorite self-promoting authors—and pick up as much spilled candy as you can!

#1
How Can I Get Fans To Read My Next Book?

Sometimes it's months before a fan gets around to reading your book. When they finish the last page, that's when they'll be most interested in your other work.

If you've sold your next book and you're signing your current release, flip to the back of the book, right after THE END, and jot a note similar to this one:

> *Hope you enjoyed reading Spike's story! Watch for my next book in the series, FIDO GOES WEST, coming this June! You'll wag your tail over the comic adventures of Spike's little brother!*

If you haven't sold a new book when you're signing your current release but still want to push your backlist, try a note like this one:

> *If you enjoyed Fido's story, SPIKE TAKES MANHATTAN is still available from PuppyPress at 1-800-555-DAWG.*

#2
Rules of Speaking Engagements

Rule #1: If you're doing a workshop, making a speech, or standing in front of a camera—wherever people might be looking at you for a while—have a copy of your book in your hands. People will tire of looking at your face and their gazes will settle on something else right in front of them—your book!

Rule #2: If you're holding your book in your hands, make sure the cover is facing out. You'll want people to recognize the cover next time they're in a bookstore.

#3
Convention-al Promotions

If you live near a city that has a convention center, keep an eye on which conventions are coming to town. Print up booklets containing a chapter or two of your book, a letter of introduction, and of course a reminder of how to buy your books. Contact the group's coordinator or the convention center's coordinator to see you might be allowed to give the group free copies as a welcome to the city. You might suggest that the welcome is on behalf of your writers' group or some other group, possibly a local charity or historical society willing to lend you their name. (This is also a great way to get rid of any old books in your inventory!)

If you've written a non-fiction book that might appeal to a specific group of people, say TRAVEL SAFETY FOR WOMEN, and a convention of businesswomen is coming to town, print up an excerpt of tips from your book. If your book is fiction, try to find a group with similar interests. For example, if you've written a mystery novel with a librarian sleuth and you hear the local convention center will be hosting a group of 500 librarians, get down there and make contact!

Remember, not everyone who works for a corporation will be sent to the convention, but those who go are expected to bring back valuable information for those left behind—and that valuable information might just include word-of-mouth about your book.

#4
It Worked for Lawrence Welk!

Last Easter, my little girls went nuts over a bubble-blowing, electric bunny in the mall. Since then, I've seen bubble-blowing Santas, teddybears, and dolls in Christmas stores. They sell for $30 or less and it's the perfect season to pick one up for your next book signing. Not all are battery-operated so they're less portable for book signings but most operate off batteries and electricity.

The bad news? After a few hours, the musical ones really get on your nerves.

The good news? Little kids notice the floating bubbles right away and drag their moms over to your book signing table!

#5
Translating Foreign Editions into Local Publicity

If you have foreign editions or translations of your book, show them off at your book signing. Fans and potential readers love to compare various language versions of books. They also like to see how other countries' artists portrayed your characters or setting on the cover. It's a real crowd-drawer!

#6
Maid Service for Writers

Angela Wisen's last book was a modest-selling romantic comedy/mystery featuring a one-woman maid service as sleuth. She did virtually no promotion except to order 500 extra copies of the book so she could send them to the media.

Unfortunately, her "advance copies" arrived after the book had been on the shelf for six weeks—too late to do any good. After a four-year hiatus, she's back to writing Maid-for-You mysteries and still has 475 copies of her last book.

For her next promotion, Angela has contacted a maid service franchise and cut a deal. Angela supplies the books, complete with a hot-pink, circle-shaped label fresh off her laser printer and offering the books "compliments of [the maid service]."

The books also contain a postcard-sized invitation to read the next Maid-for-You book, ironically due out two weeks after her planned promotion.

The maid service will leave one complimentary copy of the book in each home it services over an entire month. Their clients will never know the maid service didn't think of it themselves as a small token of gratitude for the job.

The clients get a free, funny read, and Angela gets lots of local attention from households that typically have enough funds to buy her books.

Next, Angela plans to seek out joint ventures with maid services outside her city.

#7
Getting the Most for Your Stamp

Absolutely everything that goes out of Windy Solomon's house with stamps on it goes with promotion material. That includes bills, letters to Congressmen, credit card applications, and self-addressed, stamped envelopes from his fans and readers. There's always someone on the other end of the stamp, and that someone is a potential book buyer.

Plus, if you can put your promo material inside an envelope that's already paid for, well, 34 cents saved is 34 cents earned. Or 35 or 36 or....

#8
I'll Sign Your Book If You'll Sign Mine

When signing books, take along an autograph book or a wedding reception register. While you're signing your copy of a book for customers, ask them if they'll sign *your* book.

Usually, they'll be honored. Wow. A real live author wants to know who they are.

If they're hesitant, tell them you'd like to make sure they get your newsletter or notices of your new book when it hits the bookstores.

This little book signing trick has two big benefits:

1. You get to keep their names and addresses for future use, and
2. If you're supposed to know the people standing in front of you and can't for the life of you remember their names, you can pretend to be thinking of what to write while they print their names, and you can peek and save yourself a lot of embarrassment. Just don't get caught!

#9
How To Be a Public Service

Lucy F. Butterfield self-publishes non-fiction books designed to build self-esteem for abused women. When touring with her books, she uses the abuse angle to convince radio stations to run Public Service Announcements, or PSAs, to publicize her books' value and her local presence.

The PSAs are free publicity for her, plus they have often sparked other media to cover her book signings and interview her. She always has pamphlets or stats to hand out to any reporters who show up at the signings.

"One type of promotion leads to another," she says. "I love the snowball effect!"

#10
Charitable Contributions

An anonymous author reports that his personal charity has become an unexpected source of publicity.

For several months, while writing his book, he made charitable donations in the name of his protagonist. The cash donations usually disappeared quickly and he never felt quite as satisfied as he wished. He wanted the donations to be anonymous, but he wanted to know for certain his efforts were doing some good.

He began making side trips to the grocery store to buy a bag of groceries suitable for an elderly widow on a fixed income or a young couple with a new baby. He dropped the bags at various churches in the community, each with a note saying it was in honor of [his book's hero]. Eventually the local churches discovered his identity (through the grocery store clerk!) and church newspapers featured him far and wide!

Now, when travelling on book tours, he picks up an extra bag of groceries to give to a local church.

"I have a responsibility to bless others," he writes, "and they bless me in return."

#11

Sweet Ammunition Back-Fires?

A Spilled Candy reader reports that a couple of years ago in her small hometown, an author wanted to promote her book about the hometown area where they both grew up. The author made sure her homecoming coincided with an annual festival, similar to a county fair. Her book, SWEET REVENGE, was a thinly veiled expose' of hometown secrets.

"She talked the festival coordinators into letting her set up a book signing booth and make a short speech at the festival, which draws 15-20,000 people every year," the reader says. "She had crates (!) of her self-published book sitting in the street to be bought. "

The author had thousands of peppermint candies made up to promote SWEET REVENGE. She hired a local crop duster plane to fly over the festival at its height and toss out candies to the crowds below.

"You should have seen the people diving under awnings and tables to keep from being bombed by hard candy! The festival broke up immediately, with a number of children and adults reporting to the emergency room for bruises and minor injuries. The candies that hadn't hit people shattered on the hot streets and melted. The author didn't take the time to pack her crates before she fled."

#12

A Cheaper Way to Color

Johnny the Wonder-Printer quite frequently offers advice to promo-minded authors. A cheap way to get color on your brochures, newsletters, or flyers— without paying extra for color— is to tell your printer to use whatever's left from the last job. If their last customer used green ink, you'll save the printer wash-up costs by using what's leftover.

Be warned: you'll want to use a white or cream background and you have to be willing to accept some funky-colored ink!

#13

What Goes Around, Comes Around

Everyone's jumping on the recycling bandwagon these days, so why shouldn't we?

Think of all those printouts of old manuscripts littering your office. If you're like me, you've got at least a couple of printer paper boxes of them. Mine are versions I needed to edit when I was on the road, copies my critique buddies bled on, and rejected manuscripts now mail-worn and smelling of smoke from editors' offices and gritty with shoeprints where editors, um, well, you get the picture.

So now that I have a whole forest holding up one wall of my office, I might as well get a little double duty out of recycling. Let's see how many people I can intrigue with scrap paper.

For starters, I take a more benign manuscript, use

the paper-cutter to chop the pages in half, and haul it down to my nearest daycare center and elementary school. With the state education budget being what it is, I've found that schools welcome scrap paper for the kids to scribble on. Naturally, kids take their artwork home to Mommy and Daddy who admire the stick figures and then flip the page to try to figure out what's on the reverse.

But a word of warning if you're recycling old manuscripts at daycare centers and elementary schools: make sure it's suitable for little eyes. Don't use an old manuscript that's peppered with profanity, sex scenes, blood and gore, or anything R-rated. Some small kids can read better than you think.

Another way I recycle is to use pages from published manuscripts to answer fan mail. I make sure my fans know that I'm not sending them my trash but rather, I'm being environmentally conscientious by recycling and I'm giving them an opportunity to see an actual page from the actual manuscript of the book they loved. With so many readers being aspiring authors, they've been especially grateful for the "sample."

Another sneaky way to promote your way through recycling is to use that paper cutter to turn one page into 8 little rectangles. Everywhere I used to use a Post-It Note for scratch paper, I now use a piece of old manuscript. So, if I need to jot down a phone number for someone or include a quickie message with my check for the utility bill, my "scrap" paper carries a tiny chunk of my manuscript on the back as a teaser.

Here's an example:

SHAPESHIFTER (Tedder)
"But—"
"I've found a shortcut to the Presi
Her eyes widened. "Shortcut?"
All he had to do was shake hands
imprint his molecular structure, shift
then assassinate him. The problem
to shake the President's hand, and unf
Secret Service had tightened sec
and security.

I even got permission from my employer at my day job to offer my scrap paper to any employees who need it. I cleaned out my home office, my employer's office supply expense went down, and my co-workers are very curious about my next book.

Think about it! Can you recycle and promote your books, too?

#14

Show and Tell

Does speaking in front of the local Rotary Club or women's business luncheon make you nervous? Especially when you don't know what to talk about?

"Just talk about writing and where you get your ideas," they say as if the subject isn't vague enough already.

Perhaps you've already spoken to the same groups while promoting your earlier books. You don't want to do the same ol' thing. You don't want to bore them. And, as always, you don't have time to prepare something new and scintillating.

Remember when you were a kid in school and you had Show-and-Tell every Friday morning? Well, be a kid again and share your candy.

Dig out all the material related to the writing, selling, revising, and celebrating of the current book you're promoting. Display each artifact for your audience to *ooh* and *ahh* over and tell a little about each one.

For example, in one of my last "general audience" speeches, I took the crowd through the Idea-to-Publication of my then-current book, TOP SECRET AFFAIR. Here's what I showed and told about:

*My little girl's crayon picture on the back of a recycled Government document(My audience loved this one because they had a chance to see both how I got the idea for the book and how my mind works to expand the germ of creativity.)

* An actual manuscript page, which few non-writers and unpublished authors ever get a chance to examine.

* A synopsis

* A one-page info sheet I prepared to give an editor the "manuscript at a glance"

* A cover letter/query letter

* A couple of laughable rejection letters that had the audience shaking their heads over the reasons for rejection

* A copy of a publisher's guidelines for submission

* Scribbled notes I took when an editor called to buy the book, including lots of smiley faces

* A "sanitized" version of the contract, excluding monetary amounts, my address, social security num-

ber, and other sensitive information

* A sanitized photocopy of the check, complete with dates so the audience could see that the money didn't roll in in a couple of days like it always does for make-believe authors on TV!

* Photos I sent to the art department so they could get minor details correct

* A page out of my galleys (page proofs), complete with a couple of corrections to be made

* My beautiful—if somewhat inaccurate—cover

* The complete book-just like the ones available for sale!

This particular speech takes me about 30 minutes, though it can be tailored by plus or minus 15 minutes. The added benefits? I don't have to talk from cue cards or read my speech, all eyes are on my artifacts and not on me, and I can appear calm, professional, and interesting to people instead of shy and nervous.

#15

Contest Prizes

If you're running a contest among readers or booksellers, here's a great idea for prizes. Offer a signed, engraved portrait of President Grant.

How? you ask. Isn't that a tad expensive?

Not as much as you'd think. Buy a small photo frame and fold a $50 bill so that it fits perfectly. There you have it: Mr. Grant himself, signed and engraved.

#16
Book Bonus

One way of starting a buzz might be to offer your old book as a bonus for buying your new book. That way your current fans get what they want and little something extra that will introduce them to your older work. Put a postcard in the book that asks the reader to fill it out and send it in to you (or your publisher) if they liked it.

This certainly shouldn't hurt the sales of your new work and will probably help persuade book buyers unfamiliar with any of your work to buy your new book, since they'll get two books for the price of one.

#17
Test Everything!

Just because you have a mailing list doesn't mean you have to send something to everyone on it. Test it. Send one type of promo to 10%, change a word and send it to another 10%, add or delete your photo and send it to another 10%. If something works, then you can send to the rest of the mailing list.

How do you know if your promotional campaign is working? By testing. Don't use the same exact ad or flyer for everything. Change one word. Change the headline in an ad. Change the format. Change seven or eight different things. Then see which one draws the most attention.

It's been said that 50% of the advertising dollar is wasted but we don't know which half. But we should know. If you can track what works, that's where you can concentrate your dollars. If you get 80% of your sales from referrals and spend only 5% of your promo budget on referrals, you're wasting a lot of money.

You should be looking for ways to stir up more word of mouth so you can increase your referrals because that's something that's already working. And you're not putting a lot of money into it.

When you test, don't worry about the size of the market you're testing. Go ahead and test in small markets. It's cheaper that way. When you test, you're asking the market to vote on which approach works best before you put a lot of money into it.

For example, in a flyer that suggests the reader of your book will find "fulfillment," you might change a word in your promotional material. Some people are seeking fulfillment, others are seeking prosperity, self-confidence, self-validation. See which word has the greatest draw for your audience.

#18
Prophetic Promotions

In recent years, several non-fiction books claim that ancient Biblical texts contain secret codes that predict the outcome of the human race. At least one of these books has made national bestseller lists. Some of these books have related computer programs, either fancy commercial software or limited shareware, so that the book's reader can look up their own names.

Why not see if you name or your book's name is

in THE BOOK OF LIFE? If it is, you've got a great hook to promote your work!

#19
Travel Threads

Stop fretting about looking crisp on your 10-day book tour! Stop worrying about how to fit everything into one tiny suitcase! Stop wringing your hands because your dry cleaning will never get done on time for your next appearance!

TRAVEL SMITH Outfitting Guide and Catalog offers great travel clothes for men and women on the go. They use wrinkle-free blends of natural and high-tech fibers to keep you looking fresh. Many of their items are lightweight so you won't break your back hauling luggage—and you can wash your clothes in your hotel sink. Clothes are comparably priced to business casual and tourist wear. Petite-sizing is also available. Oooh, and yes, they will even hem men's pants!

Call 1-800-950-1600 for a must-see catalog or visit their website at **www.travelsmith.com.**

#20
Talk Show Tactics

For those of you with the gift of gab (or at least, the ability to meet the press very well), don't forget to send your press releases to major talk shows and news magazines.

Watch Oprah, Montel, Jenny Jones, Rosie O'Donnell, etc, and write down the names of the producers at the end of each show (or ask a friend who's home during the day do it for you).

Don't forget to include CNN, The Today Show, Hard Copy, and any other television show that might fit your book—especially if it's non-fiction—into its daily line-up.

Warning: don't be surprised if you get a call in the wee hours of the morning. If there's a last minute cancellation of a guest or expert on a talk show or if there's a breaking news story related to your book, the producers might call you to fill the spot or provide background, whether in person or by phone.

#21
Long Distance Tip

If a bookstore invites you to visit and sign their stock, but you can't make it, never fear.

Grab a sheet of labels—either the 1x4 inch variety (usually 20 per sheet) or the 1x 2 5/8 (usually 30-33 per sheet) and autograph each label. Now the bookseller can affix the labels and sell them as "autographed" copies!

#22

Hey! Bookmark This!

Planning your own book signing tour?
Check out the resources section of BookZone at

http://www.bookzone.com

Mary Westheimer sends plenty of sweet news from her site, including a note that they offer a searchable lists of thousands of links to booksellers, book clubs, organizations, and promotional services.

BookZone is definitely worth bookmarking. They're one of the top book sites and the first one that champions the independent publishers of the world. They have hundreds of publishers associated with them, plus Publishers Marketing and Audio Publishers association sites.

If you don't need to plan a book tour, stop by and read their articles of interest to self-publishers and to any author, whether self-published or commercially published.

#23

Stressing Good Promo Ideas

Not long ago, promo wizard Vicki Hinze was faced with an identity crisis that happens to many authors. For years, she poured her promotion budget into advertising her pseudonym, Victoria Barrett, under which she writes deeply emotional love stories about healing. When her books started swinging toward deeply emotional suspense stories with romantic subplots, her publisher wanted her to use a different name to distinguish the different type of book she's now writing. The first book to bear her own name, SHADES OF GRAY, meant she had to get her "new" name out to distributors, sales reps, bookstores, and readers.

The promotional tool Vicki used for SHADES OF GRAY was a "StressChek" card. The card is plastic, very much like a credit card. The fine print instructs the recipient to hold the "Press Here" dot between the thumb and forefinger while it changes color (sort of like a '70's mood ring). The card shows four color blocks, from black to orange to green to blue, indicating tense, some tension, normal, and calm respectively.

The card goes on to explain ways to reduce tension.

The flip side of the card promotes Vicki's next book and looks like this:

WARNING:
Monitor your Stress Level while reading

Vicki Hinze's
SHADES OF GRAY

A novel guaranteed to send your pulses racing.
Read at your own risk.

#24

Classified Secrets

Author Lacy Ford uses classified ads in an unusual way to promote her novels—she lures readers to her book signings.

"When I'm planning to sign books, either in my hometown or while I'm on the road, I find out if the local newspapers offer free classified ads. Lots of papers will let you advertise something that's valued at under $150 or $100 or $50 dollars for free."

Unfortunately, many newspapers limit the free ads to non-commercial, or non-business, ads. That means Lacy can't advertise her book.

"But I can advertise myself," she says.

A typical ad might read something like this:

> **MEET THE AUTHOR!** Lacy Ford will be chatting with fans and giving away prizes Tuesday from noon to 5 P.M. at The Bookstore.

The prizes are usually novelty items such as key chains, pens from her publisher, or bags of sachet. If the newspaper decides that mentioning a bookstore by name makes the ad "commercial," then she replaces the store name with "For information, call ###-####"—the number of the bookstore. If the book signing is at a library, the newspaper never questions the "commercial" aspect of the ad, according to Lacy.

Free classifieds are a great way to publicize your upcoming book signing, particularly if the local papers ignore your press releases or insist the bookstore (or you) buy an ad if you want your signing mentioned in their hallowed pages.

#25
Better Than Cookies

What do you do with leftover promo goodies or copies of your older books that are taking up closet space? Send them to any soldier, according to Polly Franklin-Willis.

"Our military members are often sent to remote areas of the world where they don't dare leave their compounds," says Polly. "Many times, they're there without their families and after a short while, the tediousness of life there becomes unbearably lonely."

Polly notes that Dear Abby publishes "Any Soldier" addresses several times a year and various military units sometimes publish addresses to which folks back home can send care packages.

Soldiers want books, audio tapes, magazines, junk food, cookies, candy, flavored coffees, and powdered drink mixes, among other things. Look through your inventory of author copies and unused promotion material and see what you've got that might help entertain our troops, relieve a little boredom, inspire them, and maybe make life a little more comfortable. Of course, don't send anything pornographic, illegal, etc.

(Note: Due to terrorist activities, packages aren't permitted in some areas of the world. Make sure packages, not just letters, are allowed before you send off your books.)

#26
Promotion for Light-Weights

Ray Abingdon suggests sending fliers to your mailing list if your budget is really tight and you're looking for an effective campaign. Assuming you already know the flier's content, he recommends paying attention to little things that could cost you big dollars.

Check with your printer to find the lightest weight paper that won't bleed through.

"Otherwise," he says, "you'll be paying extra postage for unnecessarily heavy paper. And with the wasted money, you could be advertising to a bigger list of potential buyers."

#27
Up-Grading Your Mail

If your computer has a bar-code feature and you know the ZipPlus 4 zip code of the people on your mailing list, you can make your own address labels and improve the chances of your mail arriving and arriving on time. Even if you don't have bar-code capabilities, you can make your mail "upgrade-able."

For upgrade-able mail, you must have address quality. This means physical design, readable print, and a correct address. The optical character reader (OCR) at the post office looks for the city/state line, then the line above it. Don't put an ATTENTION line below the address and don't junk up the bottom two lines of the address with promotional messages.

The OCR interprets the characters, verifies the address with the national directory in the scientific equivalent of a split second, and sprays the bar code. Don't use teeny tiny print either. The OCR can't read print that's 14-17 characters per inch.

When the OCR scans for an address, it scans 2.75 inches from the bottom of the envelope. And, as I mentioned before, it scans very quickly—35,000 pieces of mail per hour—so yours had better be right! Leave the bar code area clear so the OCR can spray the code beneath the address. If you have a logo or an endorsement, that's okay, but put it above the delivery line.

Put return addresses on your mailings. *Correct* addresses. When fans, booksellers, publicists, etc answer your letters, they often use whatever return address is on your letter, and if it's missing some portion, a letter might not reach you.

The color of paper may cause problems, too. Black on pastels is okay, because it provides a contrast, but black on hunter green will not scan. The USPS prefers nice, boring black ink on white paper but as long as there's a good contrast, your address quality should be satisfactory.

Do you use a dot-matrix printer? Can you see the dots? If so, the OCR will have problems scanning the address.

Window envelopes often have too much glare on the plastic window. If your window is "high-glare," you can blind the OCR and it won't read. And guess what? The scanner may not read an address on an insert that doesn't fit the window envelope. Sounds silly, huh? But still a big problem in the mailing business.

If you're sending out newsletters, whether bulk, upgrade-able, or bar-coded at home, take a few extra precautions. *Do not* use staples to hold your newsletter together. The USPS will not run a stapled newsletter through the bar code reader. Think of all that expensive, high-speed equipment bought with taxpayer dollars. Do you want *your* lone staple to increase the national debt? Instead, use tape, a label, or a tab to close the newsletter.

When sending a bi-fold newsletter (such as an 8.5 by 11 inch page folded once) or a tri-fold flyer or letter (folded twice), leave the fold on the bottom and tab the open top. Why? The pricey machines, once again. The machines pull the sides open as they try to scan the address. The result? Your newsletter's in shreds and the machine's jammed.

Or try an invitation fold for your letter, brochure, or flyer. Where the tri-fold seam crosses in front, use the label to tab it closed—a real time and money-saver.

#28

"Got More?"

My friend Judith works in a Government building with about 400 other people. She usually brings her lunch and eats at her desk because she can't get to and from her home or a non-fast food restaurant within her allotted sixty-minute lunch period. Because her job as a negotiator is extremely stressful, she's not allowed to "work through" lunch. She's supposed to take a lunch break, preferably away from her desk, to keep her blood pressure down.

One day, during her lunch break, she showed up at my desk where I was stuffing a candy bar into my mouth and trying to finish a manuscript on my own mandatory de-stressor lunch break (ha!). Judith plopped down in my office, fully prepared to entertain herself by staring at me while I worked.

"I'm tired of reading regulations," she whined. "Do you have anything FUN to read?"

Not wanting to share my first draft with her and desperately wanting to work on it alone, I remembered I'd left a couple of books in my purse from an unexpected trip to the mall bookstore the night before. One was Justine Davis' futuristic LORD OF THE STORM. The other was Jill Jones' "pointy-headed romance," EMILY'S SECRET, an historical mystery about the Bronte family. I opened up my twenty-pound purse, tossed Judith the two books, and sent her on her way.

Two days later, she showed up on my lunch hour again. "Got more?" she asked.

She'd read both books in three lunch hours and a couple of evenings. She'd never heard of either author before but fell in love with them both. And she didn't typically read "that kind of book."

Did I have any more? Of course! Whenever the newspaper sends a photographer to my home, they want a picture of me standing in front of my walls (yes, plural) of books. What did she want me to bring in for her to read on her lunch hour? Meaty historical romances, not too much sex but lush with historical detail.

Had she brought back the two books she'd just finished? Uh...no. Dana had seen Judith in the lounge, engrossed in a book, and asked to borrow it. Dana now had the second book and the first one had been passed on to Becky, and Marcia wanted to borrow it next and then Wanda, then Melissa, and oh, did I mind?

The next day, I cleared a cluttered shelf on my bookcase and brought in some early Susan Wiggs novels, Delia Parr's EVERGREEN, and some of Anne Stuart's historical set. I was very careful *not* to bring in any books that were readily available at the bookstore. In fact, I couldn't find any of these at a used/hard-to-find bookstores either.

But I had a plan.

Word spread quickly that I had some really good novels in my office if anyone in the building or the adjacent buildings wanted to come by on their lunch hour and check one out—as long as they didn't bother me if I was at my desk. In less than a week, I began to hear "I've never read her books before. Does that author have anything else out?"

Funny that they'd mention that. I just happened to know those authors all had new books hitting the shelves...at full retail price. And no, I couldn't bring in one of the brand new ones to share.

Since then, I've kept a small backlist library in my office at my day job. Who's in the library? Authors who have new books coming out within the next few months.

My personal library's been a great way to introduce dozens of readers to new authors and new types of books, plus provide a little relaxation in the middle of a stress-filled day. As I've told other professional women about my library, they've started their own.

Can you, your spouse, or your friends start an office library with your older books?

#29
Fanning Out the Fan Mail

Never underestimate the importance of fan mail. Fan mail, whether glowing or even (gasp) threatening, is a good indicator of how close to home your book is hitting.

If a grieving woman sends you a tear-stained letter telling you how your book and only your book has helped her to get through her husband's terminal illness, wipe your eyes and make copies of that letter. Send copies to your agent, your editor, and your publishing house's marketing department. You want the people most likely to buy your next manuscript to know you're making an impact out there.

If fans are clamoring for a sequel to your novel, make sure your publishing house knows it. And what better way than to send them the proof?

What if you're getting hundreds of fan letters? Do you send them all to your editor? Not necessarily. Pick the best as a good representation but do let your editor know how many you are receiving.

You can have your fan mail go directly to your publisher by asking readers to write to you care of your publisher, but be forewarned: many publishers don't forward fan mail to their authors or if they do, it's months later.

#30
Sell Your Back-End

Let me clarify. Your back-end is the residual part of your business. Don't be surprised if you lose money promoting your first book, but you should be able to make it up on future books.

With future books, tell readers about your backlist. Send them to used bookstores to look for what's no longer in print or, if you can get rights back to your commercially published books, offer them through an electronic publisher or through a self-publishing venture.

If they collect all your backlist, then they're more likely to "buy new" the minute your new book hits the shelves. Your next book may not be out for another 3 months, but by the time it comes out, they've been reading your old stuff and they're dying for more.

#31
"Font-asy" Promo

"Get personal," urges author William Nation, who likes to use the personal touch in his promotions, particularly with booksellers and fans.

William sends pre-printed letters and newsletters

to booksellers and others on his "A" promotion list. He includes snippets from real and make-believe fan letters, (depending on what kind of message he wants to send), and gives them the appearance of being real endorsements by using different styles of handwriting for each quote.

When William responds to his fan letters, he uses a template (an already created letter on his computer with only blanks to fill in) and merges in the name and address of the fan, with room for one paragraph tailored to the fan's questions or comments. He uses a font made from samples of his own handwriting and prints his return letter to look as if he jotted it down himself.

If you'd like to include your "real" signature rather than a printed one on your correspondence or if you'd like to use various handwriting styles in your promotion campaign, you have a few reasonably priced options. You can buy a personalized font for under $100, with most in the $35 to $70 range. Numerous individuals on the Internet offer their services to duplicate your logo, signature, and/or an entire font based on handwriting samples you mail to them. Some will provide a signature only for $12-20. When you're ready to have your autograph copied, use your favorite search engine to locate sources by looking for "handwriting fonts" or "signature fonts."

If you're a computer geek (and I use that term very affectionately), you may want to try a software package called Fontographer, which was one of the earliest font packages available. This tool creates lots of fonts, symbols, company logo, and almost anything you can imagine for your letterhead. It's also easy to use and still one of the best font creators on the market. Prices vary with the software store, but so far, it's under $500. As of mid-2001, the price was down to $350 or so. If you winced at the price, then you're probably not a real computer geek.

If you don't have the time or money to create your very own font based on signature and penmanship, consider inexpensive font packages such as "Handwriting Fonts" by Expert Software that I still use. I chose this package because it offers 300 fonts, one of which is similar to my own handwriting, except that it's more legible!

As technology has improved, I've seen several more font creators on the market as well as available as shareware and freeware. Don't ignore the possibility of a completely free alternative.

32

The Facts of Life?

Cilla Gould's self-published booklet for teenage girls, KEEPING BOYS AT BAY, could be promoted in a number of ways. Her more traditional method of promotion is her sex education speeches at girls' high school PE classes, usually in religious schools.

The bizarre? In her single-sex workshop, she talks frankly to young teens about virginity, eggs, sperm, fertilization—you get the picture. The schools usually purchase the booklets for the girls to take home. Cilla gives them a free "sperm" to take home with the educational material.

Now, in case you're wondering, the sperm is actually a soft vinyl glow-in-the-dark snake about 8 inches long. Cilla buys 144 for less than $5 from a novelty company. From what she says, these not-actual-size samples have quite an impact on the girls!

#33
Appreciate Someone!

Say "Thank you!" to booksellers, reviewers, or other industry pro's with a certificate of appreciation, courtesy of your laser printer or hand calligraphy. For my first novel, I worked with around sixty key booksellers who went above and beyond the call of duty by setting up book signings, readers' groups, media events, and workshops. Before the dust settled, I sent each a certificate that said:

Certificate of Appreciation

awarded to:

«name»

for your generous support of
A MAN CALLED REGRET

Then I signed the certificate and either mailed it first class or priority mail or I hand-delivered it.

Not only did I receive enthusiastic replies for being "remembered," but I also cemented the relationship for future books. Plus, the booksellers hung their certificates in places of honor—where customers and employees alike will see my title and name every time they come near the cash register!

#34
A Billion and One Uses for Address Labels?

Well, that's what it seems like.

Bright, colorful labels show up everywhere. An author sends us a complimentary copy of his book and the gold sticker on the cover says "Autographed by local author."

Instead of a return address, another author's envelope bears a rainbow-colored sticker with her book's title, pub date, publisher's name, and ISBN.

A bookmark designed around the author's name has a tiny space left for a bright pink label. This month, it's a romance novel. Last month's green sticker was for a mystery novel.

Another author's fan-newsletter arrives with a red label binding the three unfolded sides together—probably much to the chagrin of the post office.

If you've got a bad case of Label envy, pick up your latest **Miles Kimball catalog (41 West 8th Ave, Oshkosh WI 54906-0001**) or at **www.mileskimball.com** for inexpensive labels or try the following companies suggested by Spilled Candy's readers (note: prices may change--and probably will!):

ARTISTIC GREETINGS/ARTISTIC DIRECT
One Artistic Plaza
Elmira NY 14925
300 for $4.95-6.95(depends on ad)
600 for $6.95-9.95 (depends on ad)
Shipping & handling varies from $1.25-1.50 per set
Colors: pastel rainbow, jewel-toned rainbow, cascading colors, metallic rainbow, blue, golf foil, white, green, silver foil, red, clear. 4 lines of print

CHECKSUNLIMITED.COM
Various designs; 200 labels for $6.95.

CURRENT LABELS
http://www.currentlabels.com/
$5.95 - Roll of 300
$7.95 - Roll of 600
Shipping & handling $1.65 under $10
Colors: rainbow, white, clear. 4 lines of print; lots of other colors and features for slightly more.

FREEADDRESSLABELS.COM
Year-round and seasonal designs

IPRINT.COM
300 labels including dispenser for $9.99

LABELS
P O BOX 3200
Salem VA 24153

250 for $4.35 (depends on ad)
500 for $5.95 (depends on ad)
Shipping and handling FREE
Colors: gold foil, white gloss, clear, rainbow gloss
4 lines of print

LITTLELABELS.COM
Color, black and white, seasonal. Free shipping world-wide.

PRINTED CREATIONS
http://www.printedcreations.com/addresslabels.htm
Variety--create your own online

THE BUSINESS BOOK
http://www.thebusinessbook.com/
or 1-800-558-0220
Contact to request a catalog.
Jewel-colored labels (2x5/8") range from $22.65 for 500 to $180.50 for 10,000, plus other types

OR

You can buy laser printer labels at your office supply store for $10-30 a package for up to 3000 labels and make your own!

#35
Sharing the Wealth

Hezikayla Rambeau suggests sending a postcard of your book cover to your list of readers and fans. Not only will the postcard announce your new book, but you can convince your reader to share it with his or her friends (and other potential readers.) Ask the recipient of the postcard to get it *signed* by five friends or neighbors (anyone not living with them) and *returned* to you for a free prize, which might be an autographed copy of one of your older books. This way, at least five other people will get the benefit of your mailing.

#36
On the Links

Do you have your own home page on the Internet yet? See if your publisher, favorite bookstores, or companies that make a product related to the topic of your book have home pages, too.

If so, link your homepage to theirs so that your readers will be able to find other homepages that will be of interest.

At the same time, ask your publisher, etc, to link to your home page. That way, a reader interested in your publisher's mystery books will discover your amateur sleuth novel. If a nursery or gardener's tools company has a home page and links to your homepage, a flower-loving customer can discover your books on gardening.

#37
Seducing Buyers by Mail

When trying to find buyers by mail, try to make each envelope look personal enough to warrant being opened right away.

Hand-write the address if you can stand the writer's cramp or if you have only a few letters to send. Use first class stamps.

For the return address, use the small lick and stick kind of labels that have flags or smilie faces and give only your address, not your name.

Curiosity is bound to get them to open the envelope. From there, a sale depends on how good the material inside the envelope is.

#38

Signing for Fewer Returns

Don't forget to sign the "stock" (the unsold books) when a book signing is over. If you're visiting a bookstore or even a grocery store that carries your books, offer to sign their copies and stick an "autographed by" label on the cover.

Not only does this discourage the booksellers from sending unsold books back to the publisher for credit (and to the author's discredit!), but book buyers are less likely to trade an autographed book at a used bookstore.

This means fewer used books in circulation. If readers want your books, then they're going to have to buy them new and at full royalty. At least, that's *my* fantasy.

#39

Ghost-Writing for Bookstores

Before your next book signing, talk to the bookseller about joint promotion. This is especially good if you're signing with a small group of promotion-minded authors willing to share creativity and expenses.

Offer to put together a newsletter for the bookseller, one that features the bookstore's name and location in the banner (headline). Ask the bookseller to write a short editorial for the front page and provide you with a picture of him/her. Each author in the group writes his or her own page, complete with photos of the author, book cover, or subject of the book. One of you should write up an article for the cover page, possibly a question/answer angle, with the focus on the upcoming book signing.

As an added bonus, ask the staff at the bookstore about their favorite types of books, and include a picture of them on the author's page that fits most closely with their tastes. They'll be more likely to help sell your book.

Try to get the bookseller and authors to agree on a share of costs. For example, the authors might put the newsletter together and pay for printing while the bookstore covers postage. Ideally, the bookseller and all authors will combine their individual mailing lists to fans and locals for wider coverage.

Also, if the book signing is scheduled for a time and location near a conference, place extra copies of the newsletter on the goodie tables or in the conference attendee packets.

#40
Bulk Rate Basketball

If you're mailing at bulk rate, says one post office employee, you'll be horrified to witness your precious bundles being thrown with the force of a champion football, but that's the way bulk mail is "sorted."

The postal worker takes one look at the state or zip and aims the bundle at a bin on the other side of the room. He hurls it toward the bin where the bundle may or may not hit its target.

So, if you're mailing at bulk rate, slip a rubberband lengthwise around each bundle. Then place a second rubberband around the remaining side.

For some reason, lengthwise first holds better and protects your bundle from getting scattered on the post office floor.

#41
Big Card

An international marketing guru told me a wonderful story from his younger days. As usual, his wayward ideas can be adapted to book promotion.

While looking for a job to support his family, he had plenty of doors slammed in his face. Some brushed him off nicely by suggesting he leave his "card" and maybe his potential employer would call him back. Then, when he began to stand out in the crowd, his luck began to change.

At one company, the receptionist behind the glass suggested he leave his business card. "Just slip it through the hole in the glass," she said.

So he pulled out his "card"—a business card the size of a small poster—and proceeded to try to fit it through the hole in the receptionist's window. His humor and innovation managed to open a door for him when only a tiny hole in a window had been allotted to him.

Maybe it's time to re-think our business cards?

#42
Speaking Tips

Forget picturing the audience in their underwear. That ancient piece of advice may still work, but only because it's meant to remind you that they have no power over you. You are the one in power. You get to talk; they get to sit there and listen. You get to impart knowledge; they get to receive.

The best advice I ever read on how to appreciate the sense of power a speaker has is to remember that awful class you had when the teacher called on you and you weren't listening or didn't know the answer. Imagine being the teacher in front of the room and calling on someone in your audience to answer *your* question. Then you'd be directing everyone's attention to that one person and all those awful, staring eyes would be off you! What a rush of power!

#43

Kid-Stealing Warm Fuzzies

Author Leanne Banks brought her fuzzy friend to a book signing at a recent conference. He was bright orange and clashed with her bright pink business suit, but every head in the room turned when he walked by.

No, not a boyfriend. Something better. Leanne's companion was a gigantic animal marionette, though I'm not sure what kind of animal it was supposed to be.

But picture this: Leanne's standing next to her cloth-draped table flaunting stacks of books. Children walking past her book signing don't notice the perky blonde in bright colors. They look right past Leanne to the fuzzy, orange monkey/bird/whatever-that-thing-is marionette, and make a bee line to Leanne's table. Mom gets dragged along. The kids "pet" the animal and Mom sees books for sale.

The marionette is a great conversation starter and attention-getter. It gives people a reason to talk to "an author" and gives the author a chance to meet potential readers without feeling on the spot.

I found a similar marionette in Lillian Vernon Corporation's Lilly's Kids catalog for $24.98 in an old catalog.

I also found a version of lesser quality in a toy store. Original price was $19.99, but it had recently been marked down to $9.99.

#44
Online Radio

Looking for radio stations that will promote your newest release? Go on-line! Try these resources:

http://wmbr.mit.edu/stations/locate

—will link you to stations with their own web pages

http://www.radio_directory.com

—will give you a by-format list of stations. If your target market likes classical, rock, country, or whatever, you can get a list of stations with those formats. Many of those listed have their own web pages or email addresses.

#45
Internet Localities

When promoting your book on the Internet, don't forget to tap into regional sales potential. You should list your book with every possible search engine or on-line directory, giving not only your book title and subject as key words but also listing your hometown and state.

#46
Newsletter Help

When mailing out your author newsletters to your fans, readers, bookstores, libraries, etc, either place each newsletter in an envelope or tab/tape the three open sides of the newsletter. The post office already requires one tab, at the center top or center middle (depending on how you fold), to keep the postal machines from eating your mail and to keep your mail from destroying their rather expensive tax-funded equipment.

Author Elizabeth Sinclair suggests using side tabs for two reasons:

1. They keep inserts inside the newsletter, and
2. They keep other people's mail outside the newsletter. Elizabeth reports finding strangers' phone bill payments and other letters inside the newsletters she receives.

#47
P.S. We Love You?

Whenever you send out a letter to booksellers, fans, distributors—anyone you want to market your book to—end your letter with a P.S.

The P.S. is considered a second headline by marketeers. Once you get a potential buyer to open your letter, if the reader ignores everything thing else in the letter, he'll read the first sentence and the P.S. Make sure both are packed with a punch.

#48

FREE Air Time!

Television and radio time can be expensive advertising for most of us. But it doesn't have to be. TV and radio stations must fill air time regardless of whether the station's marketing department has filled its advertising slots. So what happens at 11:18 at night when the station doesn't have a slot filled? Does the station black out to dead air time until the next ad slot at 11:19? No! They'll rerun their ad slotted for 10:45 or some other time. The absolute worst thing for a TV or radio station is dead air.

Okay, so they've got a few blank spaces to fill in their schedule. You've got a great ad and little or no cash. Call the station's marketing department and make a deal! Offer them a set fee per sale you make from your ad or a percentage of each sale you make if you let them run your ad "free" in their unsold slot(s). Make sure there's something in the ad that will let you know which new customers saw or heard your ad.

If the station is resistant—and many will be—remind them that they can always rerun someone else's ad in an unpaid slot and receive NOTHING extra for their trouble. And if they're worried that their running of your ad won't pull in dollars for them, let them know that because of their lack of confidence in their advertising, you're now worried that you as an advertiser won't see any new business from your ad if you paid full price. Then watch them back-track!

#49

Have a Great Day—and Buy My Book!

Travel writer Barney Burland recommends making up what he calls "Have a Great Day" cards. Basically, these are business cards that offer a happy thought, blessing, or word of scripture on one side, usually something to do with finding your way. On the back is a blurb about his latest regional travel guide and how to order it.

But Barney doesn't hand these out only in the line at the post office. He leaves them at area welcome centers and gas stations near the interstate. When he crosses a tollbooth, he pays for the 10 cars behind him and tells the toll operator to have a great day and please pass his cards along to the next 10 cars.

#50

Road Trip Opportunities

When planning any road trip that will allow you to stop at bookstores and sign stock, don't forget the book sections of K-Mart and Wal*Mart stores, discount stores that are often found in small towns where bookstores are not.

Before you hit the road, hit the World Wide Web with a few brief but very productive searches. Both K-Mart and Wal*Mart have on-line search capabilities for the addresses and phone numbers of the stores nearest you or nearest the location of your vacation, business trip, or Aunt Edna who loves for you to visit.

For example, I checked out Wal*Mart's site, which allows you to search for a given number of stores within a given distance of a given location, and found that I will pass 33 of their stores on the way to my parents' house two hours away. I printed out the list and map to take with me on my next trip "home."

To check it out for yourself, go to

http://www.wal-mart.com

and find the menu for locating their stores.

K-Mart's site allows visitors to search by state and by county. Located at

http://www.kmart.com/locator/index.htm

a query will give you a list, addresses, phone numbers, and a map for your next trip. I personally located another 20 stores on my way to my parents' house.

Uh-oh. At this rate, I might never get there in time for Mom's sweet potato pie.

#51
Turn Your Family into Walking Billboards

If you or someone in your family travels a lot, make T-shirts with your book's cover on the front and an ad on the back, such as "Ask me about my wife's book." Creative T-shirts will draw queries from fellow airline passengers, gas station cashiers, and hotel clerks. Plus, hundreds of fellow travelers will see your ad even if they don't ask the wearer about his wife's book.

You can use an airbrush artist or try to paint your own T-shirt using glitter paint—the kind found in craft stores. Or you can take your book cover to a T-shirt shop at the mall and get them to transpose a likeness of your cover onto the shirt. Some stores and print shops are able to do this with a laser printer, or with T-shirt transfer sheets for ink jet printers, you might be able to do it yourself.

#52
Name Recognition

If you're being interviewed on television or radio, don't say "my book" when answering questions. Instead, repeat the book's title every chance you can. It won't do you much good if listeners say to themselves, "Hey, I think I'll buy that bald guy's book. Now what was it called?" On the other hand, if they hear 500 GREAT PICK-UP LINES ten or fifteen times during the interview, they'll know which book to ask for.

#53
Dressing for Horror

"Uncle Scar," not his real name but a fitting nickname, is publishing his own horror novels. When he stages a book signing—and I do mean staging—he dresses in street clothes and horrific make-up. He can buy fake scars for less than $2 per bag of 2 dozen and stage blood for $9 per dozen tubes.

The effect? Well, you know how when you're sitting at a book signing table and the mall pedestrians walk right past without making eye contact? Uncle Scar doesn't have that problem. People can't help but stare. When fans of horror fiction spot him and realize why he's in costume, they stop to chat—and buy his book.

#54

Make Their Bonus Your Sale

If you've written a religious book, consider setting up speaking arrangements wherever you travel. Schedule lectures at various churches on your route. Read from your book, give a testimonial, or teach from your own material. Charge a small admission fee for your class/seminar/lecture and give away the book free.

Everybody loves to get something free! Attendees will pay for the lecture and get a bonus book, but from your viewpoint, it's the same as giving a lecture for free and selling the book. Word spreads quickly among churches, and soon other groups will hear about "that fabulous speaker we had last month" and will be ordering your book.

You don't have to have a religious book to make this tip work. Find groups willing to set up a lecture circuit for you, teach their members a little of what's in your book, and then send them home with their very own copies.

#55
Asking for Fan Mail

Whether your book is self-published or commercially published, you will probably have a short biographical sketch in the front or back of the book. At the end of your bio, add a sentence that says you love to hear from readers and then give your address. For your own safety, always use a post office box. If you live in a very small town, get a post office box in a nearby town.

Including your own address is a good promotion idea because you want to collect fans' addresses to let them know about future books you'll have out, right? Plus, many commercial publishers misplace fan mail sent "in care of" the publisher, forget to forward it, or sometimes elect not to forward your mail if they think it might offend you. Most readers won't send fan mail to an author in care of the publisher unless they feel very strongly (often negatively) about your book, but a note in your bio will encourage fans to write to you, especially if they loved your book. You might also entice them by asking them if they think you should write a sequel and if so, which secondary character should get his or her own adventures.

If you want your publisher to know about your fan mail, you can always send them copies of the most favorable letters.

#56
First Class Promotions

No matter how many times you send your mailings via what the old post office regulations called "third class mail," there's one time of year when you should never send them less than first class or priority mail.

Technically, the Christmas season isn't until Thanksgiving and runs through Christmas, but if you've got a mailing that needs to arrive in December, you need to send it by 1 November if you're not sending it first class. If you want your mailing to arrive in time for a January conference or other event, send it third class in early November or first class in December.

During the last two months of the year, the mails are clogged with thousands of first class Christmas cards and packages—which get priority over your lesser class promotional mailings.

#57
Personalize Your Newsletter

If you send author newsletters to your fans, try to include something they can incorporate into their daily lives. Make it something a little personal to you so that every time they think of it or use it, they'll think of you and your great books.

For example, if you're promoting a book aimed at working parents, you might include a quick and easy family recipe. If your book is about stress in the workplace, give a few tips on relaxation techniques or at-your-desk exercises.

#58
Establishing Your Expertise

"It takes a certain kind of person to write letters to the editor," a professor of research methodology once said. What he meant was, people who put their opinions in print aren't necessarily typical of the majority public opinion.

Katie-Jon Thomas swears it's true. A husband-wife partnership, the Thomases self-publish guides for parents of young children. Their pseudonym frequently appears in magazines and newsletters geared toward parents of preschoolers, working mothers, Christian families, baby care, elementary education, and recreation. Though they occasionally publish articles in these outlets, their strained schedule makes the best use of letters to the editor.

Katie and Jon search through relevant sections of the current WRITER'S MARKET for magazines regarding child care and parental guidance, disabilities (of children or parents), games and puzzles, general interest, health and fitness, hobby and craft, home and garden (things to do with kids), juvenile, nature, computers, religious, rural, sports, teen and young adult, travel, women's, and education.

Next, they skim the latest copy of relevant magazines at the local library (who can afford that many magazines?) and note any article that they can expound on, argue with, or offer their books as expertise. Then they write short, useful letters to the editor and fax or email the letters so they'll appear in the next issue.

Though many magazines refuse or neglect to mention the names of Katie-Jon Thomas books, these authors do establish themselves as experts by name and subject. The readers can then search them out.

#59

Insert Sales into Your Life

Rather than advertise in the newspaper, opt for a cheaper, more visible method of advertising: inserts. A one-page flyer can be inserted in a newspaper for a fraction of the cost of a smaller-sized ad.

Pick a day when the newspaper will contain few or no other inserts so your flyer will be easily noticed. Never pick a Sunday when your flyer will be lost in the dozens of department store inserts.

Most newspapers can insert your flyers demographically to hit your target market. Ask what demographics are available and decide which are best for your book.

One reader reports that her local paper charges a $60 fee to place inserts in their Tuesday paper which covers 40,000 households. All she has to do is pay for the flyers and the handling fee, and she can blanket her local market.

#60

Getting Extra Mileage Out of Reviews

Get permission to reprint reviews in part or in

full in other publications. Send your best review with your press release. Many newspapers that don't review books will run someone else's review simultaneous with a story about you or your book.

#61
Fun With Magnets

Buy magnetic stock pre-cut to business card size at your local office supply store. You can purchase a pack of 25 for about $10. If you buy in bulk or take the time the cut magnetic sheets down to size, you can save much, much more.

Peel the adhesive strip from the pre-cut magnetic card and carefully attach the photo. Use a razor blade to trim the sides, if necessary.

Send these magnetic reminders to book reviewers, distributors, or even your editor. With these promotional magnets stuck to their file cabinets, office doors, and home refrigerators, you'll keep a constant reminder in front of people who can make a difference in your career.

#62
Need Some (Non)Stinkin' Badges?

Ask an office supply or mailing service to laminate a wallet-sized photo of your book. For best results, use a laminating jacket a little bigger than the photo. Prices vary, but I found a local MailBoxes Etc that laminated a badge for fifty cents. Use a hole punch to create a pair of openings in the top, clear edge of the laminated badge so that you don't have holes disturbing the view of your cover. Use a safety pin for a fastener.

Wear the book-badge to writers' conferences, book signings, readers' conventions, Rotary Club speeches—any gathering where potential book buyers can see your cover and later recognize it in the bookstore.

Warning: Wallet-sized photos of your book cover can make attractive salesmen, but beware of the pitfalls.

First, obtain a "cover flat" from your publisher. A flat is simply the paper cover of the book, unfolded, and will show the front, spine, and back of the book. Your publisher may give you a handful or hundreds of extra flats but ask your publisher to ensure that at least one flat isn't mutilated. Some publishers punch a hole in each flat to prevent bookstore owners' returning the covers to the publisher for credit. While this practice is understandable, a hole in a cover flat can make any advertisement featuring your cover look tacky.

Next, send your publisher's marketing department a letter requesting permission to copy the cover for promotional purposes. You may be surprised to learn that cover art and graphics are copyrighted, and you may be required to pay a fee of several hundred dollars to the publisher or artist for permission to reproduce the cover, even for advertising.

Explain as accurately as possible how you plan to use the cover in your marketing campaign and that you'll use the cover in its entirety if at all possible, to include the publisher's name and logo. You should get back a letter giving you permission to reproduce the cover and under what circumstances. If you phrase your request just right, you may not be required to pay a fee. Once you get this letter of permission, make several copies of it and keep the original in a safe place.

Now, call different photo shops in your area and get competitive prices for varying quantities of wallet-sized color photos made from a print. The photo shop will charge usually $2 to $5 to make a negative from the print—in this case, your cover.

Once you've selected a photo shop, take your permission letter and an *un*mutilated cover flat or book jacket to the manager. Ask that they shoot the front cover and reduce it to wallet size. Get an estimate up front. You'll probably have to leave a copy of the permission letter with the shop in case they're ever accused of copyright violation—which could put them out of business without your letter in their file.

Decide ahead of time how many copies you'll need of each photo for your marketing project and buy in quantity wherever possible. Do shop around for price and service.

I ordered an emergency overnight job of 80 copies and paid 30 cents for each photo, plus $2 to shoot the negative. The result was worth every penny.

#63

Asking Bookstores for Help

If you're planning to sign copies of your book, put the hosting bookstore to work for you. When you set up the signing, provide a "prize" to be won by some lucky bookstore customer.

Ask the bookstore to suggest each customer register for this fabulous prize. If the bookstore is a very busy one, then perhaps the clerks could suggest customers who buy the type of book you're selling register for the prize.

For example, if the clerk spots an anthology of horror stories in the customer's arms and you're pushing your latest werewolf novel, that's when the clerk needs to say, "Have you registered for the lovely silver bullet necklace we're giving away? It was designed by horror writer, Phelan Wolfe. By the way, he'll be here in our very store in thirteen days, signing his latest book...hee, hee, hee...in blood."

Prizes don't have to be expensive, just attractive to your target customer. A prize might be a gift basket with a copy of your book and related items. For example, if your book is YOU DESERVE TO PAMPER YOURSELF, you might create a relatively inexpensive basket of goodies meant to pamper: bubble bath, a discount on a therapeutic back massage, a bag of gourmet tea, etc.

Don't forget to ask the bookstore if they'd be willing to offer a small prize as part of the package. Most bookstores are willing to pitch in a gift certificate for $10-25 or, worst case, a grab bag of books that aren't moving very well.

#64
Where to Get a Quote

Need a quote for your book but don't know whom to ask?

1. If you're lucky enough to have any friends who write in your genre or field, by all means ask them if they would consider giving you a quote. It's done all the time. Notice an author's quote on a book cover. Then look for a book by the quote-giver and see if there's a reciprocal quote from the quote-recipient. You'll be surprised—and maybe a bit disillusioned—to see how often author pals exchange quotes.

2. Ask your editor to recommend other authors who might be willing to give you a quote. If you're lucky, your editor will not only give you suggestions but will even ask the other authors for you.

3. Ask your agent (if you have one) to recommend quote-givers or preferably seek out an author whose quote on your cover or flyers will garner your book some attention.

> ***DO** query first. Send a polite one-page request for the author to look at a few pages, a few chapters, or the entire manuscript if the author has time. Your preferred quote-giver may be under a tight deadline, suffering from eye strain, picking up the pieces after a divorce, or too enamored with a new love to read anything you send. No matter how much the author would love to give you a quote, sometimes it's impossible—and for reasons that have nothing to do with your book.

***DON'T** send a complete manuscript unless the quote-giver requests it. Imposing on the author will not win you a quick quote and will probably offend the person whose quote means the most to you. This is the same as someone barging in on your writing time and forcing you to work for them. The author should feel he/she is volunteering to give you a quote rather than being forced to.

***DO** give the author a choice. Send a self-addressed, stamped postcard with your query. Allow the author to check off choices. Humor can ease the tension. For example:

( ) Sorry, but I'm drowning in deadlines
( ) Sorry, but my spouse demands all my free time
( ) I'd love to read your book! Send it right away!

***DO** send a self-addressed envelope with sufficient return postage. Even if you don't want the manuscript back, send a letter-sized SASE for your quote.

***DO** allow for a graceful "out." It's possible the quote-giver will hate your book or even you. Emphasize the author's time and let the author know you understand if he/she simply can't find time to read your book. This will allow the author the excuse of not having time and save face for both of you if the author doesn't want his/her name on your promotional material.

***DO** remember to thank the quote-giver. At the very least, send a thank you card. Even better, send a small gift. A box of gourmet coffees or a basket of local foods are nice gestures. Try to avoid alcohol and fruit cake, however. A contribution to a literacy charity made in the author's name is also good.

***DON'T** badmouth an author who doesn't give you a quote. Maybe the author will be willing or able to give a quote for your next book. But complain about an author and you may discover you're talking to her biggest fan. Not only will you be ungracious, but you'll cost yourself a reader.

#65
Sound Footing for Readers

When preparing brochures or flyers, use a "footed" font for the body of text. See how much more difficult it is to read a paragraph in this font? If you read this font for very long, your eyes would tire and your mind would wander. Make it easy on your reader.

Studies show that advertising material written in "footed" letters is 2-3 times easier to comprehend. Comprehension's more important than fancy type, isn't it? As for brief headlines, use any font you want.

#66

Everybody Loves a Parade!

Many small towns host parades, especially around spring planting, harvest time, and Christmas. Get in on the celebration by participating. You can go all out on a float announcing your name (while you toss peppermint candies to the kids on the sidewalks) or have a pal drive your convertible while you wave to fans from a car bearing a simple poster board sign.

#67

Catch the Eye with a Tense Design

If you design your book cover or you're allowed input into your publisher's plans for the cover, slant the outer letters of your title. You'll create a "structural tension" that your customers' eyes can't overlook.

Confused? Notice the sign over any Hardee's fast-food restaurant. See how the first letter, H, leans slightly outward? Now look at the last letter, S, and you'll see it also leans slightly outward.

It's so subtle, yet when you're driving down a highway, scanning the landscape for a place to stop and grab a quick bite to eat, you will pick that sign out of the clutter of billboards.

The human eye can't help but be distracted by the tension in the structure of that one word with its letters leaning away from each other. Wouldn't it be great if your potential readers couldn't keep their eyes off your book cover in the clutter of books on the shelves?

To learn more about "structural tension," read Robert Fritz's THE PATH OF LEAST RESISTANCE or any of Robert's other books on mastering the creative processes in your life.

#68
Taking a Different Route

Small press author Aleta Boudreaux sent out postcards of her book cover to invite fans to attend her informal talk entitled, "Navigating to New Worlds: Seafaring and Spiritual Journey." Aleta is the author of SONG OF THE WHITE SWAN, an epic tale of Celtic Brittany and the New World, published by Laughing Owl.

Aleta uses a different approach to book signings. She gives an entertaining, educational, mustn't-miss-it "talk" on the subject of her book at major bookstores in Mobile, Alabama. Oh, and by the way, she just happens to be signing her books there, too!

#69
Windows to Publicity

If you're contacting potential booksellers, distributors, or readers by mail, the first thing you must convince them to do is open the envelope.

If you can afford it, use window envelopes. People are naturally curious and want to know what's inside. This technique is especially effective if what's inside appears to be a check. The recipient must open the envelope to find out! You're appealing to the basic human traits of greed and fear—and of throwing out a good deal.

Of course, once they've opened the envelope, the rest depends on what enticing words you've put inside that envelope.

#70

Don't Be a Flash in the Trash Can

When sending flyers, brochures, or newsletters to booksellers, don't use neon. Blinding-bright colors have their place in the marketing world, but this isn't it.

Booksellers see lots of flashy flyers that are hard on their eyes and reek of cheap attention-getters.

Opt instead for substance over flash. Try an unusual pastel or a subtle, classy design.

Understatement can stand out in a garish crowd.

#71

Have Book, Will Travel

Nette Jolson carries a few extra copies of her older books with her on airplane trips. These are copies her local used bookstore holds for her free of charge. On her travels, she looks for passengers without books or magazines.

"The more bored-looking, the better," she says.

Then she offers them "this fabulous book I just finished and don't have room left in my luggage to carry any further." Where a fellow traveler might not accept a gift from a stranger, they will actually do a stranger a favor by taking the book off her hands.

She also looks for potential readers in airports and train stations.

#72
Advice from the Goodie Table

If you're placing promo material on the "goodie table" at a writers' or readers' conference, try to anticipate the colors other promoters will use, suggests Jack Youmans. He sees far too much bland white at general conferences, too much pink at women's and romance conferences, too much red and orange at horror conferences, etc. To catch attention, go with the opposite of what seems appropriate for the conference.

#73
Gold Boots

Several industry professionals had asked to meet briefly with me at a national conference. For various reasons, setting up a specific time and place wasn't feasible.

"Just tell me what you look like," a newsletter editor told me, "and I'll find you."

Hmmm. Sorry. It's pretty hard to pick me out of 500 conference attendees. I'm not 6 feet tall with flaming red hair and a chain-mail mini-skirt skirt. I'm not a 5'2" Playboy beauty. I don't have a Z-shaped scar on my forehead or horns parting my hair. Call me ho-hum, but physically, I blend right in with the crowd.

Since I'd be changing clothes several times in several days, I couldn't say, "I'll be the one in the purple polka-dot dress." Footwear was another matter.

"I'll be the one in the gold boots," I told each conference contact by telephone or e-mail.

Each day, I wore a different outfit with my short, gold boots. My contacts discreetly checked out the feet of the 500 conference attendees and spotted me easily.

Not a bad idea, I've decided. I've attended readers' conventions where a well-known author or women's fiction was pointed out among fans as "the one with the interesting jacket" and male literary author as "the gentleman with the lion's head cane."

Me? I'm the one with the gold shoes.

#74
Shhhhh—The Library Secret

If you've published a religious/inspirational book or a genealogy/history book, don't overlook the library market. In fact, get to the nearest library as fast as you can and ask to see a library directory.

The American Library Directory, for instance, lists about 30,000 libraries and categorizes them as public, educational, religious, and special, plus a few other descriptions. You'll find hundreds of church or religious college libraries to buy your SERMONS FOR THE ORDINARY MAN Look carefully through the listings under each state and you'll find markets for A HISTORY OF THE GEORGIA FRONTIER.

But don't stop there—special libraries exist for ethnic literature, medical texts, and lots of other types of books.

#75

The Envelope, Please

At a regional conference, an author who didn't want to be identified gave me a bright-colored #10 envelope for all my conference receipts. The front looked like a spreadsheet, listing various meals, airfare, hotel, parking fees, gas, rental car, etc. with blanks for 5 days and a total column. On the side, the author had listed her upcoming books.

Unfortunately, she said the promotion wasn't working very well. She was trying to publicize a very funny little book to a bunch of very serious, literary-type writers. However, this promotion would be perfect for books geared to business people attending a conference on the same subject as your book.

#76

Sneaky Authors Strike Again!

Unless you're already a Big Name Author, you probably won't see your books in airport bookstores—unless you put them there yourself!

John Wolverton, a rocket scientist (really), recommends placing an extra copy of your book in each major airport you travel through. In the back, place a "Time to Re-order" card inside the book and leave the top edge of the card sticking out. The card should be of colored cardstock (we suggest pink or a deep beige) and contain ordering information such as shown in the example below.

When a customer takes the book to the cash register, the cashier will see the card poking out of the book and the words "Time to Re-order" and pull the card. Hopefully the shop manager will think the book has sold well (hey, last copy, right?) and re-order.

TIME TO RE-ORDER

TITLE:
How to Tame A Pilot
AUTHOR:
Trudy Sandlin James

PUBLISHER:
No Regrets Press
28 Dugan Lane Ste A
Cornerstone GA 00000

PRICE: $5.99
ISBN: 0-00000-000-0
PHONE ORDERS:
1-800-MARRY ME

SUBJECT:
How-to guide for women who want to marry pilots

#77
Stand Out in the Crowd

Stand out at a gathering, whether it's a writers' conference, a book signing, or a convention. If you're on the shy side, you won't have to jump up and down to be noticed because your conference attire can help you break the ice.

Maybe you're the distinguished gentleman in the gray beret. Maybe it's an unusual jacket. Maybe it's a different, loud Hawaiian shirt every day. Maybe you're the lady in red—from head-to-toe.

The object is to be noticed and remembered, at least during the life of the gathering so that people can seek you out or point you out with ease.

Do make sure your gimmick is appropriate for the subject of your book. Otherwise you may not be taken very seriously if you show up in a robber's mask to hawk your book on financial investments.

#78
The Radio Shuffle

First time on the radio? Put your notes on 3x5 or 4x6 index cards. You'll be able to shuffle the cards quickly without the microphone picking up those pesky sounds of rustling paper. It's okay to use note cards, especially if you're nervous, but it's not okay to be obvious to your audience.

#79

Who Is This "J" Person?
And why is he sending me bad photocopies?

A California author is happy to share this tip, but it works so well, he wants to remain anonymous! He's self-published several how-to-succeed-in-business books and gleaned this nugget from a seminar on marketing your small business.

This promotion-minded author clips a favorable review or newspaper article about his book and makes hundreds of really awful but still readable photocopies. At the bottom of each one, he writes a can't-miss-me note with a thick marker. Usually, he says something like, "Saw this and thought of you—J." or "You've got to read this! —J." He figures most people know someone whose first or last initial is "J."

Then, he haphazardly folds the paper, staples it, and hand-writes the address—keeping that mysterious personal touch. He lives in a major city and travels frequently so the postmark is not a dead giveaway that "J" is really the author.

#80
Increasing Your Mailing List

At a major writers' conference, I attended one workshop along with about 200 other writers. As we entered the meeting room where the workshop was held, we were asked to form two lines and sign up for a special prize to be given away. Or we could drop our business cards into a huge goldfish bowl.

The author presented the workshop at a dozen other workshops of similar size all across the country. At each, 200-plus people happily gave up their addresses. She did have one fabulous prize to give away, but she drew the winner's name from a pool of all workshop attendees.

As a result, she had several thousand prime names for her mailing list when she turned her workshop into a how-to guide for writers.

#81
Trick or Treat?

Mary Hasty, an obviously beloved elementary school teacher who self-publishes collections of regional folklore, gets well over 200 trick-or-treaters every Halloween, many of them current or former students. This year, she handed out extra special treats.

Mary printed small cards (single-fold, similar to thank you or invitation notes) on her home computer and black and white laser printer. Mary punched a hole in the upper left corner of each card and tied lollipops to it with colorful yarn.

On the outside fold, she typed in large letters: A SPECIAL TREAT — A HALLOWEEN BEDTIME STORY JUST FOR YOU. Inside, in much smaller type, Mary printed a 250-word Halloween story from the 19th century, meant for the child's parents to read aloud at bedtime to put the little ones' fears to rest. At the end of the story, Mary asked parents to look for her upcoming book, this one on folklore for children.

"I'm giving out the candy anyway," Mary writes. "I already have the note cards in my desk drawer, plus the yarn in my sewing basket. So all this really cost me was the time to print and package, and I did most of that while watching TV."

And the icing on top?

"I didn't have to go to my market—they came to me, and all on one night."

#82

Hotel Hints

Paul Hamlin suggests making friends with the management of a hotel chain. Business travelers are always looking for something interesting to do and by the second or third night of a trip, they've already finished the paperback they started on the plane.

"The hotel management might let you put out copies of your last book in their lobby or even in their rooms. Make sure the hotel guests understand the books are compliments of the hotel, but make sure, too, that you put a sticker inside the book to let guests know to watch for your current or your next book."

The type of hotel you approach depends on the type of book you're pitching. Find out what type of guest the hotel caters to (business travelers, vacationers, upscale, family, etc) before making a deal.

#83
Fictitious Newsletters

Joan Pendergrass hopes to sell a funny mystery series soon and is already planning her promotion strategy. She has a newsletter in mind, but not like any we've seen before—thank goodness! (Just kidding, Joan.)

"You know those bothersome letters you get every Christmas from long lost friends and relatives?" Joan writes. "They're either brag-fests or totally boring, but they're very informative. Where else would you get to find out that Uncle Hal's dentures turned blue permanently because his little grandson had been playing around with food coloring? Where else would you find out how Aunt Sally discovered the secret herb she puts in the Thanksgiving stuffing isn't the plant she mail-ordered from a gourmet cooks' catalog but that Hal-Junior's friend had been smoking dope and hid the evidence in her herb planter?"

Joan plans to send a "personalized mimeographed" Christmas letter, featuring her mystery series protagonist, to bookstores, fans, reviewers, and distributors.

"Except," she says, "I plan to make it funny."

#84

Leaving Her (Book)Mark

Polly Franklin-Willis sent us a bookmark cleverly disguised as a business card.

Everywhere she sees a bulletin board that allows businessmen and women to tack up their cards, Polly leaves a bookmark. These bulletin boards are usually located wherever people have to wait in line a long time.

So far, she's left her bookmark-card in post offices, restaurants, restroom hallways, service stations, drug stores, grocery stores, print shops, message boards at convention centers, fitness centers, welcome centers, discount stores, and bars.

#85

Uses for Used Books

Check out used bookstores for copies of your older books. See if they'll make a deal so you can pick up extra copies of your backlist cheaply. Give away the books or sell them at your cost when you give a workshop on the subject of your book or on writing.

#86

Captive Audience?

Take bookmarks with you everywhere you go. Leave them with your tip at restaurants. Drop one onto the countertop in the post office. One author who asked not to be identified carries a roll of tape and a pack of business card sized bookmarks everywhere, then tapes a bookmark at eye-level in airport restrooms.

#87

Here's to Success!!

All over the country, booksellers are lifting their coffee cups to their lips and thinking, "Hmmmm, I wonder if Susan Wiggs has a new book out yet." Think of it: their eyes are barely open, their minds are still foggy with sleep, and yet they're starting their day with thoughts of an author and how to sell her books!

If you study Susan's career (historical romances, romantic historicals, and even a children's book), you'll see how this Harvard grad's marketing savvy has boosted the popularity of her novels. Booksellers seem to adore her, whether or not they're drinking from her promotional coffee cups.

In 1994, when Susan was promoting her historical, CIRCLE IN THE WATER, (Harper), she sent an advance copy to Harriet Klausner, a respected reviewer. Harriet ended the glowing review with the words "Live the Adventure! Read Susan Wiggs."

Every morning over coffee, booksellers are reminded of the adventure Susan's novels promise. On one side of a plain white coffee cup is "Live the Adventure!" On the other side is "Read Susan Wiggs."

She ordered approximately 100 cups through a novelty promotions company for about $2 each, including the rush job and shipping. The following Christmas, Susan sent cups filled with Hershey kisses to extra special booksellers as a reminder of her upcoming historical.

#88
"Dear Librarian" Cards

If your book is coming out in hardback or trade paperback size, you may find acquaintances reluctant to spend $12-25 for your book. Once T.J. McNeil sees that first wince of resistance, she gives them one of her Dear Librarian Cards.

Her D.L.C.'s are business cards which ask if the librarian will please support local readers' interests by ordering copies of her book. She gives a tiny synopsis, title, author name, ISBN, and price.

And of course, she puts D.L.C's in every piece of correspondence she sends out.

#89
Sticky Notes" and Sneaky Authors

They're affectionately known as "sticky notes," and the most recognized brand is 3M's Post-It Notes. They come in pastels—mainly light yellow— and eye-catching neons. The best size for self-promoting writers is the 1.5 x 2 inch size.

Before you head to the bookstores to check on the sale of your books, arm yourself with a pad of sticky notes and a pen. You can wait until you're actually in the bookstore, but we recommend you write notes when nobody's looking so bookstore customers won't think you're odd. There's also the risk that you might offend a bookseller—a definite no-no.

A simple note will do: *Great book!* or *Fabulous read!* or *Couldn't put it down!* Strip the note off the pad and stealthily stick it to your book cover.

A personal note stuck to a book will get it a second glance and very likely convince a customer to pick up the book for an even closer look. Also, customers will assume the note is from the store manager or a patron in the know.

As a test, I hung out in a K-Mart to see if these phantom endorsements would really help sell books. I placed one note on one book in the rack of six. (I knew the author and honestly loved her book.) Customers read the cover of the book with the note on it and then bought a note-less copy, leaving the endorsement to catch the attention of the next book browser until the last copy was gone. I repeated the ploy once a day for the next 2 days—until K-Mart sold all 24 books in stock in 3 days, leaving dozens of other authors' books in the racks around it!

#90

1-800-BUY-ME!

Check with your publisher to see if they have a toll-free number for orders, whether by bookstores or individual readers living in the middle of nowhere.

Then print the 800-number, along with your book's title, your name/pseudonym, ISBN, release date, publisher name, and book price on *every* piece of promotional material you send to bookstores and readers.

#91
Condensation?

Got a non-fiction book you're self-publishing? Turn your book into an article!

Take one chapter or a part of one chapter and spiff it up a little bit, perhaps with a new introductory paragraph or different examples. Send it to a magazine or trade journal that caters to your target audience.

For example, if you've written a book of tips for working moms, you might alter the chapter on leaving dad with the baby while mom's away on business. If the article gets pubbed in a major magazine for parents or working moms, hundreds of thousands of potential buyers will learn about your book.

#92
Blue Light Specials

Here's a great idea from Jill Jones, author of EMILY'S SECRET and CIRCLE OF THE LILY. Jill and fellow St. Martin's Press author Haywood Smith, organized a five-day "Thelma and Louise Book Tour" of Southern towns—in a LeBaron Convertible Turbo, no less!

Besides bookstores and interviews, they decided to experiment with unscheduled KMart stops. They were so successful, we want to urge all promotion-minded authors to give this idea a try next time you're travelling.

1. If your book is currently in bookstores and you're on the road, stop by every KMart you see in every town you drive through.
2. Go to the book section of the KMart and see if any copies of your books are still on the shelves.
3. If so, go the store managers, introduce yourself with a big smile, and tell them you'd like to help them sell some of your books.
4. Ask if they'd like to do a "Blue Light Special" on your book. They don't have to offer a discount, but you'll be available to autograph the books and talk with customers for the next hour/30 minutes/etc.
5. If the store managers agree, give them a short blurb to incorporate into their PA announcements. Include your name, book title, a brief synopsis of the book, whether you're a best-seller or award winner, and any unusual tidbits, either about you, your book, or your setting.
6. If Mother's Day is coming up, have them remind their customers that your book would make a great gift for Mom. If Christmas is coming, then your book would make the perfect stocking stuffer. If you're months away from a good holiday, well,

> an autographed copy of your book would be a terrific birthday present for the guy or gal who has everything.

The benefits of this kind of promo?

Even if KMart runs out of copies, customers have heard your name and title and can probably find your book at local bookstores.

KMart managers may ask that the number of your future books be upgraded. Make an anonymous call to the local newspaper to "tip off" that a real live author is signing books and meeting fans at the local KMart.

Try to schedule your stop for a busy time—Saturdays, the night before Valentine's Day, etc. You'll meet more fans that way, and of course, you'll get the names and addresses of your fans for your mailing list, right?

#93
Up, Up, and Away!

Okay, it's a bit pricey, Vernon Balcher, but hey, it's BIG! Draw attention to your book signing or conference booth with a giant custom inflatable balloon!

This multi-colored, cold air balloon is 23 feet high and features your logo or your message (MEET THE AUTHOR!) on a removable banner. The balloon has its own fan for easy set-up. Shipping and handling is $129, plus CA sales tax. For more info, call Calico (the company name) at 707/448-7072 or fax 707/446-8273 (last known number).

Oops! Did Vernon forget to mention the price? $1,899.00.

#94

"Oh, Sure, You Can Make a Copy . . . . "

Margaret Brownley is the queen of gimmicks, and her "Hogs Head Gazette" is an incredibly popular, incredibly cheap, incredibly resourceful gimmick for promoting her RIBBONS IN THE WIND and other novels for Topaz.

The Hogs Head Gazette is a front and back flyer designed to look like an old-timey newspaper. Margaret cleverly uses humorous "news stories," lists, and ads. Her "A Woman's Guide to Safe Motoring" and "Women at the Wheel, Circa 1915" are hilarious.

And the best part? The Gazette is so funny that readers make their own copies (saving Margaret the expense!) and pass them on to other readers who make more copies!

Consider Margaret's brainchild and see if you can start your own promo Ponzi scheme!

#95

100% Great Publicity

Author Sharon Ihle wrote us and mentioned she had a sure-fire winner of a promo idea and she was keeping it top secret until the next reader/bookseller convention. Of course, we had to see it for ourselves.

Sharon gave her readers and favorite booksellers a tasty treat—a KitKat wafer inside a pale red wrapper.

On the top of the candy bar wrapper is the title of her book, TEMPTING MISS PRISSY, her name, a sketch of the saloon-owner hero, and the fact that she's the award-winning author of THE MARRYING KIND and THE BRIDE WORE SPURS.

On one side of the wrapper is a note from Sharon, saying she loves to hear from her readers and to contact her by mail or e-mail, along with the addresses.

On the other side is basic information on her book, including the publication date, publisher, and price.

On the back, Sharon invites her readers to visit her home page for excerpts and upcoming titles, then parodies the typical candy bar wrapper with the following:

NUTRITIONAL FACTS	Daily Values	%
Hero	Tempting	100%
Heroine	Feisty	100%
Humor level	Side-splitter	100%
Thrill level	Spicy	100%
Happy Ending	Forevermore	100%

#96

Follow-up on Your Past Promotion

Follow up on your contact with readers, booksellers, and distributors. One mailing might or might not hook them, but 1 out of 4 will "buy" on a repeat mailing. Haven't you ever received a letter and put it aside or forgotten about it and then been reminded of it when you got a second follow-up letter? Your follow-up could even be a thank you letter or a how- did-you-like-the-book letter.

#97
Personalizing Your Mail

The U.S. Post Office has made lots of upgrades, technologically speaking. Barcodes, self-adhesive stamps, and free Priority Mail envelopes are some of our personal favorites.

Or maybe we should say impersonal favorites.

Author Cheryl St. John promoted BADLANDS BRIDE, a Harlequin Historicals lead title, with a personal touch—courtesy of her local post office.

"My local post office has special cancellations that run for thirty days," Cheryl reports. "In February we had the President Ford birthplace. The likeness of Ford was about 2 .5 inches high—a real eye catcher."

That's right. Get out your ruler and measure off 2.5 inches. Takes up a nice corner of an envelope, doesn't it?

Impressed yet?

The recipient of an envelope bearing that kind of stamp is going to give that letter a little better treatment than the usual flag, LOVE, or flower stamps, don't you think?

"The postmarks vary in size, too," Cheryl says. As of Cheryl's letter, the special cancellations were for College World Series and for Breast Cancer Awareness.

"The College World Series is about 2 inches by 4.5 inches long, including the logo, date and postal station."

Sounds like that kind of eye-catcher would be expensive but it isn't. Not if you normally trek down to the Post Office and pay for first class postage anyway.

"The pieces are hand cancelled, so they will only take fifty pieces without charging. Any over are five cents each." Cheryl's secret? "I take fifty a day until I have my mailing out."

Cheryl advises calling your main post office to ask for information. At her main post office in Omaha, she gets her cancellations at the international mail counter where they sell collector stamps, pins, etc.

#98

Translating More Publicity with Libraries

Do you have extra copies of your book that you can't read because they're in a foreign language?

Maybe you can't even identify which foreign language?

Many commercial publishers send you "author copies" of your book when it's translated and sold overseas. After selling 5-10 books and receiving dozens of foreign copies, your closet may be bursting at the cracks.

You can't throw them out. They're your words, whether you can read them or not.

So what do you do with spare foreign copies?

Keep one copy of each foreign translation and take the remaining copies to the nearest library. Large libraries often keep foreign translations for specific groups who are learning English as a second language and want to read American books comfortably in their native tongues.

Have someone snap a photograph of you shaking hands with the head librarian as he/she accepts your generous gift. The library will want to notify its non-English speaking patrons of new books in other languages, and you'll want to send a press release to a few newspapers to let them know about your donation—and your newest books.

#99
Tiny Posters

Delia Parr, who writes exquisite historicals for St. Martin's Press, always has such wonderful promo ideas for her books!

When I last saw her in New York City, she was sporting eye-catching pins on her lapel, each pin featuring the cover of a novel she'd written. Of course, I had to know how she did it, and Delia was more than willing to share her secrets for a subtle, classy promotion campaign.

Delia says that each lapel pin resembles a postage stamp that measures about 1" by 1 1/2". In fact, for her previous novels, she used pins sold by the post office as commemoratives for postage stamps and altered them to show off her book cover.

"I ordered the blank pins from a supplier," says Delia of her more recent experimentation with lapel pins. "I take my cover to Kinko's and have it reduced to 25%

(full color) and then laminated. I cut it to fit the pin and then simply glue on top with craft glue. Voila! Instant pin."

Instant pin, instant promo, but not instant expense. "The whole thing can be made for about $5," according to Delia.

#100
Ta-Dump, Ta-Dump, Ta-Dump, Dump, Dump

If you've always thought of a "dump" in a negative way, it's time to stop. You know those impressive point-of-purchase displays you see in bookstores? The cardboard mini-bookcases crammed full of Stephen King's last dozen bestsellers? Maybe there's even a life-size cardboard cut-out of a cover model or celebrity attached to the bookcase? Well, that's called a "dump." And according to author Barbara McMahon, you need one for your book signings.

"Ask for old dumps from book stores," advises Barbara. "Cover them with information about your next book, and have them at the stores the days you do signings. That way you can have your books to one side for those customers who might be too timid to approach 'an author'!"

Barbara's already obtained a dump for herself, and she put it to good use at the over twenty book signings she scheduled in one year.

And one more bit of good news: dumps fold easily, so you can slide them into your trunk and haul them to all your author appearances.

#101
Money Talks

Not long ago, I was browsing in my favorite clothing store. I was a regular customer there and until that day, I had bought most of my business wardrobe off their racks. You see, my day job required that I dress a certain way, and unfortunately for my bank account, even "business casual" wear was too casual.

As usual, the manager wanted to chat while I shopped. And as usual, she wanted to talk about my writing career.

"I'd really love to read your book," she gushed, as if I could miss the hint. She wanted a free copy and she wasn't even a relative.

"Hmmm, I think the bookstore across the street still has a couple of copies left," I told her. The library had copies as well, but hey, another 6% in royalties was another ...21 cents.

The manager wrinkled up her snippy little nose and her upper lip curled up until I could see her gums. "I didn't mean I wanted to buy it."

Funny, but nothing I tried on that day seemed to fit. All I could think was "As much money as I spend in your store, you could be giving my books away at the door!"

I went home feeling unappreciated as a customer and unsupported as a local author. But no sense wasting negative energy over the incident. I decided to do something about that lack of respect my long hours of writing received.

At some point in time, I'd been caught in an office supply store during a thunderstorm (as if it takes much reason to keep me there) and had decided I couldn't live without several packages of 4x6 rose-colored, unlined index cards. Finally, I had a use for them.

I had seen local teachers' unions try to get respect for the dollars they put into the region's economy by designing their checks with an extra line or logo so that the recipient knew where the money had come from. I wanted to let my local community know what writers add to their coffers.

I wanted local businesses to know how much we support them financially and that once in a while, it would be really nice if those businesspeople would support us, too.

I started the card with a headline: *This purchase made possible by...a romance novelist.* This could just as easily have been a mystery writer or a how-to expert but the book the store manager had snubbed as something she would read for free but wouldn't buy was a romantic suspense novel so I chose to emphasize the romance.

I added the next line, *Support your local authors—we support you*, to show a direct relationship between their support (financial or otherwise) and my patronage.

Since I didn't have a book coming out in the near future, I listed my last book plus a few of my critique buddies' books.

The results? Mixed. The dry cleaner I'd frequented for years turned up his nose at my card. That's okay. My new dry cleaner loves getting my business.

When I'm late for work, I whiz through my local

Hardees for a biscuit and give them yet another of my Money-talks cards. If they get 5 cards in a week, yes, it means I'm late for work a lot, but it also means they're getting my business.

Like it or not, now they know there's a local author right under their noses and they see my name and book titles every time I buy breakfast. About 75% of the people who get my card rave about it or think it's "cool." The rest are ambivalent or snooty, which serves not to depress me, but to flag which businesses won't get my support in the future when other businesses might be more willing to support my books.

Here's what my latest Money-talks card looks like:

This purchase made possible by...

a romance novelist.

Support your local authors—we support you!

Lorna Tedder

Access:
Book One of The Lorelei Files
Spilled Candy Books for the Next Millennium,
January '99

The Cure for Shyness
Kensington Books,'99

For more information,
visit me at www.lornatedder.com
or ask your favorite bookstore!

Bonus Section

to help you promote your books online

Bonus Section Table of Contents

The following 5 articles are by Jim Daniels of JDD Publishing. Jim's site has helped 1000's of regular folks profit online. Visit http://bizweb2000.com for FREE "how-to" cybermarketing assistance, software, manuals, web services and more. No time to visit the site? Subscribe to Jim's Free, weekly BizWeb E-Gazette: freegazette@bizweb2000.com

Article A

"Need More Orders? Fix This..." by Jim Daniels

After 3 years online I found a mistake that instantly increased my orders by 20%...

Last month I learned a few more valuable lessons about doing business online. I didn't know it, but I was committing a mistake that was costing me thousands of dollars each year.

I really should have know better actually. I've been marketing online since 1996. And I've been told by many folks that I have a good grip on how to do business online.

What's that old line, "physician heal thyself?" Well it applies here. Three years is a long time to be making the same mistake at my web site. But that's how long this had been going on.

So what are these horrible mistakes I had been making for so long?...

I thought you'd never ask.

I've been pushing away potential customers by dragging them through more trouble than necessary at the most crucial time during their visit to my site — right when they were ready to place an order!

Actually, I refused to truly acknowledge the problems until I was forced to reckon with them. I had received a fair amount of complaints from potential customers who had trouble ordering at my site, but the complaints were well spaced out so I figured it was just part of doing business online. Then again, most problems you tend to ignore until something brings them to a head. That's what happened at my site just before the holidays...

It all started when the third party web site that processed all secure orders from my site essentially went dead. Along with it, my orders all but stopped. When the company (which shall remain nameless for their own protection) could not get the ship righted in a few days, then a week, then two weeks, I finally smartened up and took action.

And what started as a real pain in the you know what, ended up as a blessing in disguise.

After investing lots of time and a little money, I have increased the orders being placed at my site by a full 20%. Without generating extra traffic. That's a lot of money, especially over the course of a year. Scratch that, especially over the course of THREE years!

As any webmaster knows, the lifeblood of your business online can be the secure ordering process you offer to your customers. So when my secure ordering system shut down, the last thing I thought it would be was a blessing in disguise. But that's just what developed. The lessons I learned were invaluable. I only wish someone else had suffered them and wrote about it in their ezine first! :-)

Anyway, here they are. Don't take them lightly...

Lesson #1 and 2: You absolutely MUST keep the secure ordering process at your website simple, streamlined and fast. If at all possible, offer a one-page, secure checkout for your customers. And you may not really need that shopping cart!

My own example elaborates on this perfectly...

First, here is the "Old Way" I accepted secure orders at my site: (Bear with me, this is a bit tedious...)

My old secure shopping cart system took customers through no less than four separate web pages before they were done ordering. At each page they would enter some information.

Page one was off my site altogether, was not secure, and resulted in scaring away about more people than I realized. From there shoppers who were bold enough to continue had to click the "checkout" button to go to the secure area. (If they accidentally clicked "continue shopping" they were brought back to my site instead of to the checkout page.) If they DID click the correct SSL checkout button they moved to the secure area. That is, IF their ISP kept them on the same server. If not, and many ISP's do not, their cart was reported as empty. Bye-bye customer. The surfers who made it to step three usually continued through and placed their order.

Sounds sloppy right? Well believe it or not, many shopping cart providers have inherent problems similar to these that you do not learn about until you've invested too much time or money.

For this reason, I strongly suggest you take a look at your site. Do you really need a full blown cart? Maybe not. If you are selling a small number of items, the answer may very well be no. You could actually do much better with simple stand-alone order forms. I certainly do! Just take a look at my..."New Way" to accept secure orders at my site:

The surfer clicks "Secure Order" and is immediately brought to a secure order form in the SSL area of my server. The form is a single page which lets the buyer complete their transaction in one step. Done. Order placed.

To see this simple setup in action, click to any "Secure Order Form" at my software catalog.

The nearly instant 20% increase in orders has taught me (the hard way as usual) that web surfers want a simple way to place their secure order. They cannot be bothered with learning how to use your cart or clicking through too many pages. The quicker you get them in and out of your checkout process, the more likely they are to complete the transaction.

It makes sense really. Have you ever walked out of a store because there was only one register open and the line was too long? Well that's what you are doing to your web surfers if you can't give them a speedy checkout process, or express line

And I learned one more lesson from all this...

Lesson #3: Think twice before you hire any third party company to provide a service that you may be able to perform without them. This applies especially to something as crucial as processing your orders.

There are many things that webmasters hire third party companies for. But things like web site maintenance, product shipping, credit card transactions and the like, may be very simple to do in-house. In most cases you'll find software that can automate or at least simplify most tasks so that they can be handled without a third party provider. Not only will you save money doing this, you will also have the peace of mind that comes along with depending less on other companies.

If you are just setting up shop online this lesson will really help you save money and aggravation in the long run. If you already have a web presence, make a commitment to sit down and evaluate it. Can you pull things in-house that are being handled by other companies right now? Even if it means shelling out cash for your own merchant account or SSL server space, you may be very glad you made the move some day.

That's not to say you should never hire other companies online. Undoubtedly you will need to hire SOME web services that are just too costly to do in-house, such as web hosting or real-time processing providers. But the fewer third party services you employ, the less likely you are to be left in a compromising situation that is beyond your control. And that's not good if it handicaps your ability to do business online.

So take some time and learn from my mistakes. I promise to keep making them as long as you get something from them!

Article B

"Your Freebie"... Giving it Away FREE, With No Strings. by Jim Daniels

In order to make money online, there is one thing you absolutely MUST do. You must motivate people to read what you have to say. Whether it is your email message or your web pages, if they don't read it, you don't make money.

There are lots of ways to accomplish this and I've tried quite a few.

Among all the methods I've tried, one stands head and shoulders above the rest...

It's called "Giving something of value away for free."

Here's a perfect example of this in action:

When you saw the title of this article, were you curious as to what the "freebie" was?

Did it give you that extra incentive to investigate a little further? Hey, you've read this far haven't you? It must have been somewhat effective.

Well, rest assured, this web page does include a special freebie for you. Unlike most articles at my site, the article itself is not the only freebie. I'll get to your freebie in a minute though. First I want to elaborate a bit on this marketing ploy called the freebie.

How many times have you tried a free magazine subscription? How about a free month of internet service? Ever receive a free laundry detergent sample in the mail?

If you didn't answer yes to at least one of the questions above, I'd be very surprised.

You see, these big companies know the power of "free".

Do you think they would go around giving their stuff away for free if it didn't pay off in the long run?

Hey, even if you never subscribe to that magazine, sign on with that ISP, or buy that brand of detergent, these companies have accomplished an objective. You have tried their product and heard their name. Perhaps you even were impressed by the fact that they gave you something for free.

The bottom line is that "free" works in marketing, especially on the Internet.

Now, of course you can't go around giving everything away for free. **However you can and should be giving away something!** Of course it has to be something of value.

Whether it is a free subscription to your email newsletter, a free software program, or something else of value, if you give it away for free (with no strings!) people will remember you.

Okay, now I'll practice what I preach. Here is *your* freebie, just for reading this article...

I have something very special for you today. I just finished a new e-book. It is designed for newcomers to internet business. I have no plans to sell it. Instead, I will be giving it away for free. (I had second thoughts after I was done - it came out better than I expected!)

Anyway, I just uploaded it to my site and the link is below.

One note before you download it though...

This e-book is a bit unusual. There's a special twist to this e-book. So that I may help you with your own "freebie" strategy, I have written it in a somewhat "anonymous" fashion. I did this for two reasons...

1. I did not want the book to look like blatant self-promotion - it really is a completely free e-book with no strings.

2. I figured if I wrote it in this fashion, other webmasters may be interested in giving it away at their site. (It reads like it could be from any successful webmaster.) My only benefit from this would be a few links within the book that point to my articles. These active links are just a few among dozens of excellent resources.

Okay, visit http://www.bizweb2000.com if you wish to see this book and download it..

Remember, if you like it, feel free to re-distribute it. I think you'll find it makes an excellent free gift. And you may be pleasantly surprised how many people will remember you for your freebie!

Article C

Are Your Email Messages Good Looking? by Jim Daniels

"Good looks" are very important in an email message. This is often overlooked by many email users. It is a fact that an email's content is diluted greatly if the message itself is "not good looking."

Have you ever received an email message that looks something like this...

Thank you for requesting more information about our services! We here at ABC Company would like to present a special offer to all of our cherished customers.

There are two main reasons why email messages turn out looking like this. Although the reasons are quite simple, many email users don't understand them.

Reason number one is called line length. When composing email, most people just type and type without using a hard carriage return. If it looks fine when you're done, your email program probably automatically wraps the words in a nice legible format. This word wrap is usually done based on a line length of anywhere from 70 to 80 characters.

Well, let's say I receive your message, but my email program doesn't have the capability of automatically wrapping incoming messages. Since you performed no hard "end of line" carriage returns when typing your message, my email software thinks it's one long sentence. Now your nice, easy to read message looks like that example above.

O.K. So how do you avoid this problem? Simple! When composing email messages, use a hard carriage return before you get to the end of each line. I have found that a maximum line length of 64 works to alleviate this problem almost completely! Of course, you'll always run into an instance occasionally, depending on your recipients' settings, but this should do the trick 95% of the time!

Another reason people encounter "funny looking" email messages is called proportional character fonts. Like I mentioned earlier, all email programs are different. Therefore the fonts used by each program varies widely. Basically, there are fixed pitch fonts like Courier (found on Eudora) and there are proportional spaced fonts (like AOL and Compuserve email).

With fixed-pitch fonts, all characters in a paragraph will line up directly above each other. With a proportional-spaced font, CAPS, space bars and other keystrokes are wider, so each line is a different length. The bottom line is this. If you create a message using one type of font and send it to an email recipient using the other, the message will not look the same when they receive it!

Once again, the solution is simple! By using a hard carriage return before the end of the line you can keep these problems caused by the difference in email programs to a bare minimum. If you plan on sending the same message to multiple recipients, or attempt any drawings, consider testing the message with a friend on another service.

There is a third way for your email messages to look bad. Although it is far less likely to happen, you should be aware of it. Many word processing or text editor programs allow you to save a file as another format. (Such as ascii.) It may look great to you, but when sent via the Internet it can become scrambled.

You may have received one of these messages at one time or another. They are easily recognized by the repeated "U" characters in the text. To avoid this problem, simply use the cut/paste or copy/paste method to extract text from a document in other programs.

The last thing you want is an email message with great content, being dismissed simply because it wasn't "good looking" enough.

Article D

"My Biggest Online Marketing Mistake" by Jim Daniels

Did you ever make a mistake without knowing it?

As a person who firmly believes in learning from my mistakes, I've made it one of my goals, every few months or so, to pause long enough to look back through my endeavors. Not so much to reminisce, but to consider carefully, the steps I've taken to get where I am today. When doing so, I carefully analyze every online marketing tool and method I've tried over the past few years.

Not only does this process help me to decide the path of my future online marketing, it also allows me to better assist others. By passing along some of the important decisions I've had to make, I can help others who may be coming to the same forks in the road, or simply passing through similar learning curves.

As I think back to my early days of setting up shop on the internet, (a few years ago) I can recall at least one very big mistake I made. To this day I see lots of other folks making this very same mistake. Perhaps you are one of them.

What is this mistake I am so willing to own up to?

Without a doubt, I waited too long to start building my web site.

When I started my business I had no idea how to even begin building a web site. The web authoring programs you see on the market today were still taking shape. There were a few on the market, but they were clumsy and difficult to use. For nearly six months I went on trying to grow my online business without a web site.

I used email marketing exclusively. Although there weren't nearly as many ezines back in early 1996, there were enough to survive on. I placed classified after classified and submitted articles every week in hopes of drumming up exposure.

Oh, sure, it was a good lesson on the importance of email marketing, but I was really missing the boat. All I had for a web site was a few free web pages that came with a couple of reseller programs I had joined. I figured, hey, that will have to do.

After all, I was making money. More money than I had been making at my regular 9-5 job. But, making money without a web site of my own was actually both good, AND bad. It was good because it helped me shed my day job so I could really focus on honing my internet marketing skills. But it was bad because it clouded my judgement. I figured hey, who needs a web site if I can make money without one? (How naive I was!)

Once I decided to make my living online, I finally smartened up and decided I should have my own site. And it was THIS decision that turned out to be one of my best. Yeah, I know, those of you with your own web sites already, are thinking c'mon Jim, THAT was one of your best decisions? Sounds like a no-brainer to me!

Well, to you, I say look around. To this day, this decision remains as one of the biggest obstacles for many would-be cyberpreneurs. Let's face it, there are literally millions of people settling for free space on someone else's server and calling it their "online business". Don't get me wrong, there's nothing wrong with putting up some free pages to drum up some traffic - for YOUR OWN site.

The simple fact is, if you are at all serious about making enough money in cyberspace to change your lifestyle, you need your own web site and your own domain-- <www.yourcompany.com>. This is one of the biggest and best decisions you will ever make for your online business.

Sure, it can be a big undertaking, and that is exactly what keeps most people from doing it. Just remember, every great thing you achieve in life and business starts with a single first step. That step is getting started. Don't make the mistake I made. I figured, "Hey, I don't have the time or know-how to build a great web site that gets thousands of visitors a week."

Instead, do what I did after I smartened up:

Get your own domain name and put up a decent home page and two or three informative web pages to go with it. Once you accomplish this goal, add a page or two every week. Before you know it you'll have a super informative web site consisting of hundreds of web pages - the kind of site that attracts visitors and in turn, makes sales.

You can start today by checking to see if the domain name you want is available. This URL, http://www.virtualis.com/vr/jdaniels/, will help you do that.

Once you settle on a domain name, reserve it and it's yours forever. Next, get busy building your web site. For a list of software titles that will aid you with this task, go to http://www.bizweb2000.com/webmastr.htm.

Once you have a few pages built, get them online! This is the start of your REAL internet presence. You'll add web pages constantly but the key is to get something up!

Remember, don't make the same mistake I made and limit your income by waiting too long to get your site going. Get busy TODAY building a real cyber-home you can be proud of - YOUR OWN web site!

Oh yeah, and one more thing... Before you select a host for your site, read our free report on web hosting — The Bare Facts... at http://www.bizweb2000.com/virtual.htm.

Article E

"The Cyber Two-Step"
by Jim Daniels

Everyone always wants things wrapped up in a neat little package. Although this is impossible when it comes to online marketing, I'm gonna try today.

"The Cyber Two-Step" is dedicated to the literally hundreds on internet newbies who have asked the following question "I'm putting my small business online. I have a very small budget and want to know how I should go about setting up an effective internet presence".

My answer? Simple. Do my version of the "Cyber Two-Step".

Here it is...

STEP ONE - Email

Make email your number one priority and start your email marketing campaign as soon as you have a product or service to offer.

Be sure to use a good email program like Eudora. You can get the freeware version at http://www.eudora.com or the Pro Version for around 39 bucks at most software stores. Learn how to use every feature in it, as it will become your best friend in your cyberbusiness. It will let you do things like publish an email newsletter, send targeted email to thousands of prospects and gather and store information on every subject imaginable.

Put your email marketing campaign into action right away by seeking out email newsletters related to what you will be marketing. You'll find resources for locating these at The Direct Email

List Source http://www.copywriter.com/lists/ .

Once you find some of these newsletters, do three things...

1. Subscribe.
2. Write and submit articles.
3. Buy advertising.

This is the just the beginning your "email marketing strategy". It will eventually tie in with your web site but it is important to get started marketing right away, even if you do not have a web site yet. This will help you generate income while your site is being built and launched.

Beware: Along the way, you'll be tempted to try unsolicited bulk email. Don't do it. Use only targeted email marketing and never send email to someone who does not want it.

Once you have your email campaign underway, the next important part of your email marketing strategy is to stay in touch with your customers and prospects by publishing a weekly or monthly newsletter via email. In it, offer free valuable information.

An ezine is an excellent tool in promoting your products and services. Publishing your own ezine is much easier than you may think. I suggest you spend a great deal of your allotted time and effort on this important facet of your marketing campaign and start an ezine right away. Even if your web site is not ready, start an ezine. It will be the perfect vehicle to help launch your site when it is ready. For some ezine publishing resources, read the article at

http://bizweb2000.com/contact.htm

STEP TWO: The Web

Once you've established your email marketing campaign, you must put up a web site. Not just any old site, but a site with content consisting of at least 80% free information about your area of expertise. The other 20% can be about your products and services.

If you have no idea how to build a web site, either hire someone who does, or train yourself by selecting a program at http://bizweb2000.com/webmastr.htm and sitting at your computer until you become a webmaster.

Once you get the hang of webmastering, start building your site. If you're not sure where to start, stop by my home page [www.bizweb2000.com] for some ideas. Notice how the information is presented. If you offer valuable information for free, people will be happy to read about what you are marketing, and many will buy.

Some other integral parts to remember about the step two:

A. If you are serious about your web campaign, get your own domain name, or www.yourcompany.com.

Without your own domain, you have a strike against you from the get-go. Use our search banner at the top of http://www.bizweb2000.com/freehelp.htm and find out if the name you want is taken. If not, reserve it right away.

B. Be sure to offer secure transactions at your site. Accepting credit cards is a MUST if you plan to make money in cyberspace. Getting a merchant account for your business is no longer a difficult task. Once you have it, set up a secure order taking system at your site.

C. Promote your web site constantly. People will NOT find it by accident. You must use resources like search engines and links with related sites. To learn how to get strategic links visit http://www.bizweb2000.com/linking.htm and try the recommendations there. That stuff works. How do I know? I wrote it, and my site now has over 1000 other sites linked to it.

D. Keep expanding your site. Constantly add new pages. The content can be tips, articles, or any other item of interest to your web site patrons. The point is, just keep getting bigger. The bigger your site is, the more people you can reach, especially through the search engines. Growing your site is a never-ending task. Commit a day a week to it and your business will grow along with it.

Well, that's it for today's lesson. Now that you know the Cyber Two-Step, get out there and start doing it!

And remember, if you have any valuable feedback, our new CyberMarketing InfoBoard is open 24 hours! Come on by and get in the conversation.

Also Available from Spilled Candy Books for Writers

RECLAIMING THE MAGIC:
A WRITER'S GUIDE TO SUCCESS

by Lorna Tedder

Get back on your feet after your career hits a brick wall.

ALL ABOUT WRITING TO SELL:
A BESTSELLING WRITER TO WRITER GUIDE
TO THE CRAFT, BUSINESS,
AND SECRETS OF GETTING PUBLISHED

by Vicki Hinze

This book gives you down-to-earth advice and backstage secrets to the business and life of being a writer. To get as much information elsewhere as you'll find in this 115,000 word guide, you'd have to buy dozens of books on the writing craft, publishing business, contract negotiation, personal philosophy, and advice for dealing with all the problems inherent to a writing career. No one non-fiction writer's guide anywhere covers this much information in friendly, easy-to-understand language. Bestselling author, lecturer, and writing teacher Vicki Hinze is at her best in this important addition to any writer's electronic library.

Also Available from Spilled Candy Books for Writers

**BOOK PROMOTION FOR THE SHAMELESS:
101 MARKETING TIPS THAT REALLY WORK**

by Lorna Tedder

Our bestseller to date! Lots of wild and crazy ideas for promoting your next book—from real, live authors!

**BOOK PROMOTION SAVVY:
ANSWERS TO A NEW AUTHOR'S QUESTIONS
ABOUT MARKETING AND PUBLICITY**

by Lorna Tedder

Basic book promotion advice for the new author as well as the multi-published bestseller.

**ADVANCED BOOK PROMOTION
FOR THE SHAMELESS:
MORE MARKETING TIPS
FOR PENNY-PINCHING AUTHORS**

by Lorna Tedder

Advanced book promotion techniques for self-promoters who've been around the block a time or two and need fresh ideas on what works and what doesn't.

Order Form

Dear Spilled Candy,

I'd like to order the following:

____ print copies of **RECLAIMING THE MAGIC**
at $17.95 each for a total of ....$_____

____ disk copies of **RECLAIMING THE MAGIC**
at $12.95 each for a total of ....$_____
PDF? RTF? HTML? Disk or E-mail?

____ print copies of **BOOK PROMOTION FOR THE SHAMELESS**
at $11.95 each for a total of ....$_____

____ disk copies of **BOOK PROMOTION FOR THE SHAMELESS**
at $9.95 each for a total of ....$_____
PDF? RTF? HTML? Disk or E-mail?

____ disk copies of **BOOK PROMOTION SAVVY**
at $9.95 each for a total of ....$_____
PDF? RTF? HTML? Disk or E-mail?

____ disk copies of **ALL ABOUT WRITING TO SELL**
at $19.95 each for a total of ....$_____
PDF? RTF? HTML? Disk or E-mail?

____ disk copies of **ADVANCED BOOK PROMOTION FOR THE SHAMELESS**
at $14.95 each for a total of ....$_____
PDF? RTF? HTML? Disk or E-mail?

____ print copies of **ADVANCED BOOK PROMOTION FOR THE SHAMELESS**
at $14.95 each for a total of ....$_____

Subtotal $________

Add $3 postage for print or diskettes $________
Sales tax (Florida residents—6%) $________

Total amount enclosed $________

Please send payment to:

Spilled Candy Books
P O Box 5202
Niceville FL 32578-5202

Or fax to **850/897-4644**

Name:

____

Address:

____

City/State/Zip:

____

E-mail Address:

____

To Pay by Visa or Mastercard,

Cardholder's Name:

____

Card Number: ________________________________

Exp Date ________________

Cardholder's Signature:

____

Printed in the United States
5529

9 781892 718389